Praise for *Reverberate!*

This book takes verbal skill building to a whole new level! I love how Kate Peters breaks down the issues and answers into manageable steps. Her examples are interesting and filled with insights.

If you want to have authentic communication and make sure your message is heard, you need this book.

- Laura Browne, Author of *Interview Speak: What Your Interviewer Really Wants to Know*

The definitive book on communication, including both the theory and how to make it happen. While I have known Kate for a long time, and she helped me be better in my endless communication needs at that time, it is really her understanding of what is necessary in a business environment to get things done (Reverberation) that has stuck with me into my retirement. Read every word - there are gems to uncover in each paragraph, and usually a great story to go with it.

- Mike Sternad - retired CFO

Reverberate!

The Art of Finding Your Voice in a Noisy World

By Kate Peters

Library of Congress Control Number 2026903271
(978-9-69-789279-2 Hardcover)
Library of Congress Control Number: 2025927914
(978-9-69-7892778-5 Paperback)

978-9-69-789279-2   Reverberate! Case Laminate Hardcover
978-9-69-209388-0   Reverberate! Dust Jacket Hardcover
978-9-69-789277-8   Reverberate! Paperback
978-9-69-789278-5   Reverberate! eBook

Book design by Rick Schank of Purple Couch Creative

Dedication

This book is dedicated to my husband, who is my running mate, and friend, Doug Simao. His steadfast belief in this work and ongoing support has been vital to my journey. It is his voice in my head that tells me over and over again to keep going when the going gets tough. There are no words to express how grateful I am for his encouragement, relentless insistence, his love, and generosity. The world is a better place because he is here, and I am a fortunate person to live my life with him.

Table of Contents

INTRODUCTION

TWO DEGREES, ONE PASSION

The request was simple enough: A CEO of a major corporation had lost his voice and needed help getting it back. It has always surprised me that most people know so little about their voices. Most of us are dependent on our voices to get through the day, but as was the case with the CEO, we ask our voices to do a tremendous amount of heavy lifting on a daily basis. We then wonder why we get hoarse or can't sound the way we want to when we speak or sing.

On this beautiful spring day, while gazing out the window at my garden, I thought about the request and the simple answers I had found to his problem. I didn't realize at the time that solving his problem would end up being the pivotal point not only in my professional life but also in my personal life.

Let me give you some background information about myself and how I ended up receiving that phone call. I graduated from Pitzer College and Cal-State Fullerton with two degrees – a Bachelor of Arts in psychology and a Master of Music in applied voice. I loved both subjects, which is why I devoted so much time to them, but I was worried that the world would be a little less enamored of them – at least from the practical feed-yourself and keep-a-roof-over-your-head perspective.

Despite my initial doubts, and to the great relief of my parents, I managed to make a living as a musician and actor using my degrees. It could be attributed to following my passion, or maybe I was just in the right place at the right time. Nevertheless, I was able to strike a balance between pursuing my love for the arts and meeting the practical demands of earning a living wage.

As a professional classical singer, I regularly performed and taught voice to singers and actors. Surprisingly, I used my psychology degree quite a lot in this capacity. A little knowledge of human behavior helps when trying to get people to break habits or convince them to practice. Since I didn't tour much, I was able to start a family. My daughters were exposed to music from the beginning, as they heard me singing while they were in the womb, and as young children, they played under the piano while I was teaching voice lessons. It was an excellent way to live until it came to an end in divorce.

I should also note that parenthood — and unfortunately divorce — is another instance where knowledge of psychology is helpful. Any parent will attest to the fact that a good knowledge of psychology is essential for the healthy upbringing of children ... and any divorcee will tell you it can also help in maintaining mental stability during the dissolution of a marriage.

During that difficult time, as a single mother I sought out other sources of income and realized my skills could be helpful in the business world. My first opportunity to explore this arose when a student asked me to assist him with a business presentation. Although I had never worked with PowerPoint before, I approached it as content to be delivered, like a song or the lines in a play. I paid attention to rhythm, pitch variation in his speaking voice, contrast in his ideas, and the overall impact of the narrative. I found the entire experience fascinating, and it also proved successful for him. As an artist, I wasn't sure how to do more of this, so I didn't immediately pursue it, but the approach lingered in the back of my mind.

At that point, I was well-established teaching voice to singers and actors. My mission was clear: To help individuals find their voice and confidently take the stage, showcasing their best and making the most of their talents. I was making a positive impact by helping people improve their skills, and I found it personally fulfilling. So, when my soon-to-be-second husband suggested I might be able to help some of his business clients, I didn't immediately see the feasibility. Sure, there was that one student I helped with a presentation, but the business world? The prospect seemed remote.

I would later learn that there are strong commonalities between the corporate world and the world of the arts – big egos, incredible talent, relentless drive, and a need to engage – but at that point in my career this opportunity was so far removed from my typical clients of broke actors and high maintenance singers that it might as well have been science fiction. And then came the phone call.

The CEO, we'll call him Dave, was definitely in vocal trouble. When he returned home each night from work, he could barely speak. His problem wasn't a medical issue per se, and it wasn't because he was traumatized by the stress of his work or even the hours he kept, though they were long. He simply had no voice left to share. At the end of each day, he literally could barely speak. It took a full night's rest to restore his voice enough to take on the next day of work. And so, the cycle spun ever downward. As a consequence, his family was feeling isolated, his marriage was on the line, and there was always a risk that he wouldn't have a voice on the next analyst call.

It didn't take long to discover Dave's vocal folds were spent. Long days of talking on the phone, giving presentations to his organization and the board were taking a toll on his vocal stamina. In the voice world we call that vocal fatigue, and when we met the first time, I knew exactly what he needed. If he had been a singer or actor, we would have met in my studio and worked at the piano. Instead, we met at a table in my husband's offices. Instead of asking him to sing for me, I asked him to give a presentation with which he was comfortable. And instead of giving him scales and vocalises to work with I gave him a pitch pipe and some instructions for how to use it to find his median speaking pitch, a suggestion to hydrate more, and some guidance on practicing the techniques we discussed. Within a few short weeks, Dave's voice issues improved, and I gained some powerful insights along the way.

First, I was surprised to learn that as a practitioner of the arts I was in many ways better prepared for the corporate world than countless business professionals. Conventional wisdom, backed by very real economic and academic institutions, taught the opposite – that is, that the skills needed to succeed in business are the opposite of those needed to succeed in the arts. The myth suggests that people best suited for the business world have MBAs, only read non-fiction, and have no need for the skills taught in the arts. Yet here was Dave, a powerful CEO whose career and life were on the brink because after decades in business he didn't have the skills that any theater major would have gained in a few short years of stage work.

Second, the demands of his work were similar to those

of a stage performer. Granted, an actor typically doesn't have to analyze financials or devise risk matrices, although those would be useful skills to add to a degree program in the arts. The CEO, however, must routinely contend with the intricacies and nuances of a live performance. In fact, a business leader is always 'on stage,' literally and metaphorically.

Dave was a charming, charismatic person with a lot of what we call "Executive Presence" who had worked hard to be where he was, but once we got past the vocal issues, I could see more areas to increase his impact. We began to look at the consistency of Presence, how actors foreshadow what they want an audience to take away from their performance, and how sound patterns help an audience follow what we say. We even delved a bit into content, such as storytelling and aligning stories with intent. This gave me great insight into the power of "why" in communication. I began to see how all these areas, when aligned, can create impact far beyond mere charisma.

And, finally, I learned that my arts-centered education and career were anything but impractical. Skills that I took for granted – standing with confidence even when you don't feel secure; walking into a room with poise and energy despite being exhausted; composing one's thoughts while under pressure; making sure one's voice aligns with the words being spoken (or sung) – were desperately needed in the corporate world. I came to realize that my education and background, my successes and failures, my experiences and observations, all merged to create a unique body of knowledge. My two degrees (plus 10,000 hours) aligned with my one passion: Helping people find their voice.

A DESIRE TO CONNECT

Following my work with Dave, my thinking on the impact of communication evolved. I developed a methodology to work with people other than artists, and conversely that methodology influenced my work with performers. However, the world evolved too. When I began this work both artist and businesspeople were more likely to "stand and deliver."

Over time the type of requests I received from clients changed. Rather than asking how to give a keynote speech or sound like an authority, clients began to ask how to inspire, and now professionals want to engage their C-suites and C-suites want to engage their organizations, much as performers want to engage their fans. The desire for impact was shifting away from being driven by a need to succeed.

Eric Haseltine, a futurist and neuroscientist, says this desire is part of human nature and will grow in intensity as the world increases in complexity. Where once great orators sought to sway audiences with their ideas, leaders today seek to communicate in ways that connect. A great example of this is the first time a President of the United States included a surprise guest at his State of the Union address.

Historically the State of the Union began as an eloquent evening of oration presented for members of Congress and a few other dignitaries. Beginning in 1927, it was broadcast over the radio; in 1947 it was televised; and in 1965 it was moved to prime time – a true indication of the significance of the event for all citizens. By the late 1970s the audience included everyone in the world with a television, and President Ronald Reagan, a former actor whose Presence always aligned beautifully with his message, would soon discover a new Intention for the event – to connect more deeply with the American people so they would be more open to his ideas.

In his 1982 State of the Union Address, President Reagan invited an average American to be his honored guest and sat him next to Nancy Reagan, the First Lady. Lenny Skutnik was a federal worker who, two weeks earlier, had rescued a woman from the Potomac River after a plane crash. Lenny knew he was considered a hero, but imagine his shock when President Reagan called him out in his speech and described him as an example of "the spirit of American heroism at its finest." The story was gripping and people watching felt pride and connected with Lenny. He could have saved them or one of their neighbors or even one of their children.

Having Lenny there seemed to transform the event and the people on camera. Reagan was known for his charismatic Presence but bringing in an average American seemed to take the President down from that rarefied state and expose his humbler attributes which helped him more fully connect with the people watching.

At the time the President needed the American people

to accept a plan that would take work to implement so he introduced Lenny by saying:

"Yes, we have our problems; yes, we're in a time of recession. And it's true, there's no quick fix, as I said, to instantly end the tragic pain of unemployment. But we will end it. The process has already begun, and we'll see its effect as the year goes on.

We speak with pride and admiration of that little band of Americans who overcame insuperable odds to set this nation on course 200 years ago. But our glory didn't end with them. Americans ever since have emulated their deeds."

After Lenny was introduced, the crowd jumped to their feet, giving him a standing ovation. Reagan then went on to talk about other everyday heroes.

"Don't let anyone tell you that America's best days are behind her, that the American spirit has been vanquished. We've seen it triumph too often in our lives to stop believing in it now."

It worked so well that every President since Reagan has included "Skutniks," (everyday heroes honored in the speech) in their State of the Union broadcast.

I am not implying that leaders today need to be actors, although it served Reagan well. I am saying that Reagan brought it all together and is a good example of how this works. He had an Intention to connect with his audience during his talk so that people would be willing to roll up their sleeves and work together to put his plans into action. He had a great story to back up his ideas about the average American being important, and he had terrific Presence.

Until the mid-2000s, most businesspeople never expected to have to show up on a video or a JumboTron when giving updates, nor did they have to think about connecting in the way they do today. But here we are. Some companies even have television studios, and their executives get hair and makeup done by professional makeup artists before their all-hands meetings. Then, of course, there is a universe of social media giving average people far-reaching platforms to become influencers from the privacy of their homes and others the ability to comment, sometimes making or breaking reputations. The challenge becomes: In this brave new and noisy world, how can leadership voices rise above the crowd?

What I have learned through years of experience, study, and practice, is that our ability to influence and have impact is NOT about attractiveness or status, although those may have a supporting role to play. Instead, it forms at the intersection of three key components of communication: Intention, Story, and Presence. The better aligned these are — the better they reverberate with each other and resonate with the audience — the more significant the impact.

CREATING REVERBERATION

When sound strikes a surface, it's reflected at varying times and amplitudes, creating an echo which conveys complex information about the sound, the physical space through which it travelled, and the source from which it emanated. This is reverberation as we traditionally understand it. In this book, I expand the concept of reverberation beyond auditory harmonics and discuss it in terms of the dynamics that govern effective communication. It is the result we are striving for when we align Intention, Story, and Presence.

But there's more, and this is personal. I have come to realize that what drives me in my work and in my life is a conviction that the world would be a better, more peaceful place if the people in it could convey their thoughts and feelings more effectively. In my profession, I have chosen to work with executives because it's their job to influence others. If I can help leaders become better communicators, I can then impact their organizations. Their organizations, in turn, impact their communities, their industries, and the world. There are people with ideas everywhere at all levels of companies and societies who want to be heard – hence this book.

If you want to learn how to make a sincere connection with others, then you've picked up the right book. Inside these pages you'll find principles based on research, application, and experience. You'll find stories and answers as well as tips and techniques that will help you align Intention, Story, and Presence, creating Reverberation and enabling you to connect and communicate more effectively.

THE COMMUNICATION ALIGNMENT MODEL

Intention drives **Story,** delivered through **Presence** and all work together to create **Reverberation:**

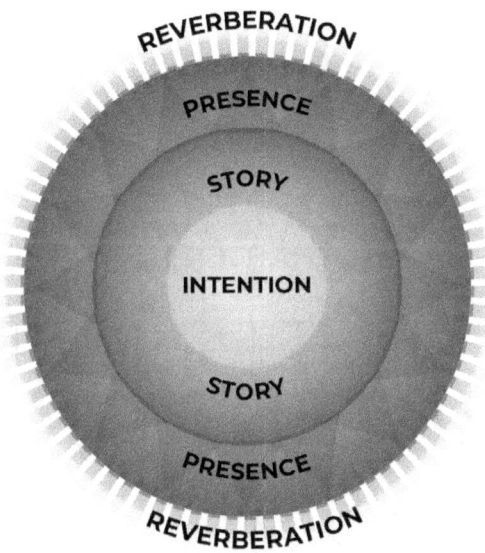

When these elements align, your message resonates with clarity, trust, and emotional connection. When they're out of sync (e.g., powerful content delivered flatly, or strong Presence without purpose), your impact weakens.

Be warned: This book involves change. It involves being honest with yourself about who you are and what you are trying to accomplish, being steadfast in your resolve on how to get there and owning the consequences of your actions. It involves breaking old habits and creating new ones. Be aware that such journeys take time. I am pleased to be part of yours.

Oh, and Dave? He found his voice, healed his marriage, and led his company to great heights.

CHAPTER 1

THE FIRST PRINCIPLE, INTENTION

*"The human voice is
the most beautiful instrument of all,
but it is the most difficult to play."*

– Richard Strauss

WHAT YOU WILL LEARN

CHAPTER 1: INTENTION

Why you say what you say — and how it shapes everything.

What You'll Learn

- What Intention really means in communication.
- How Intention influences tone, delivery, and perception.
- The neuroscience behind reading other people's intent.
- Why Intention is a superpower when aligned with authenticity.
- Practical tools to clarify and express your Intention in every interaction.

Key Takeaways

- Intention is always present — being aware of it makes you a more powerful communicator.
- People pick up on Intention instantly, often unconsciously.
- When Intention is clear and honest, it builds trust.
- Aligning Intention with action is the foundation of your voice's integrity.

WHAT IS A VOICE?

The human voice is an incredible tool, demonstrating the capacity to convey a wide range of emotions and thoughts. At its core, it represents our ability to communicate, a skill that has evolved over millennia. The fact that we can speak at all is due to the tenacity of evolution and our fierce desire to communicate with each other. From simple sounds to the formation of complex languages, the human voice has become one of the most sophisticated and diverse forms of communication in the animal kingdom.

More than its literal meaning, the concept of voice is a powerful tool for self-expression. Writers often speak of finding their voice, a unique identity that encompasses language, writing style, perspective, and tone. Finding one's voice is a journey of discovery akin to a dialogue with nature, wherein the environment speaks to us, and we feel compelled to illuminate it through our unique human perceptions. I am reminded of Pablo Neruda who once commented that his poetry "took its voice from the rain, and like the timber, it steeped itself in the forests."

In the world of music, 'voice' refers to the various parts sung by singers in a choir. Soprano, alto, tenor, baritone, and bass blend their voices to create the achingly beautiful sounds in Morten Lauridsen's emotional "Lux Aeterna." 'Voicing' also extends to the various lines of music played together on the piano, contributing to the dancing synchronizations in the contemporary music of Stevie Wonder, Billy Joel, and Alicia

Keys. It's the arrangement of pitches in a chord or harmonic entity. For a piano, 'voicing' is a mechanical procedure, the gentle manipulation of the felts surrounding the hammerheads as a tuner coaxes a darker tone or brighter sound from the instrument.

As we learn to play with music, we start by making strange, scratchy, and weak sounds. We explore each one with dedication, discarding some and nurturing others, discovering new sounds, reprising the old. We persevere through the uncomfortable experience of not knowing how to create what we want to hear. We listen closely to others to discern a style or emulate something we like. We play with motifs and experiment with phrasing, knowing we can learn from others while anxious to finally make our own music and find our unique musical voice. Like the whole of English literature, which is built upon the variation of 26 letters, music is a universe of possibility built upon a finite number of variables.

I find the human voice beautiful, and I hear music in spoken words. Voicing words, we produce pitches and rhythms, tempos, and dynamics. Finding one's voice as a speaker means recognizing the uniqueness of our voice as a complex instrument. And if our voice is an instrument, perhaps we are the composer creating an original work consisting not only of sound but of our perceptions of the world around us and our reflections of the world inside us.

Voices intone the arc of our life story through expression,

inflection, pace, and articulation. They vibrate to the rhythm of our environment and culture. They hum our relationships and our values. They are the melodies we have heard and the harmonies and dissonances we have designed or adopted. They play a person's life just like a song or a theatrical work of art. They are how we interact with the world around us. They are how others hear our story and how we enter the conversation. As we pass through life, we become adept at using the instrument of our voices. On a day-to-day basis we create compositions with our voices and our words, weaving stories, expressing sentiments, declaring positions. Sometimes we do this improvisationally, saying something on the spur of the moment; sometimes we do so with extensive forethought. It has been my experience that in all these instances, from spontaneous to deliberate, there is always an inherent motivation, a drive, a purpose for our compositions. I call this Intention.

UNDERSTANDING INTENTION

Defining the word intention seems like it should be an easy task. A dictionary definition might read something like this:

in·ten·tion. *(ĭn-tĕn'shən).* Noun. An aim that guides action.

But even as we read it, we sense there is something more. It's such a simple yet powerful word. Intention haunts us when we lack it; vexes us when we misunderstand it; elevates us when we achieve it. When it comes to communication, it's one of the most formidable tools at our disposal. It's everywhere − everyone has it and everyone expresses it. The problem is, we often do not recognize our Intention much less the impact it has on others.

Intention is always present, whether we know it or not. People perceive it without even trying. It stands to reason, then, that the clearer we can be about our Intention, the more authentic we'll show up. Fortunately, Intention is something we can work with to make it more genuine to ourselves and more obvious to others.

PERCEIVING AND EXPRESSING INTENTION

Years ago, I was coaching a Senior Vice President. She was receptive to coaching and a lot of fun as a client, but she took a disliking to the word "Intention." In her mind, "Intention" was related to a wish. She preferred concepts like "purpose" or "goal." She couldn't wrap her head around the idea that Intention was none of these things and yet all of them. The common expression, "the path to hell is paved with good intentions" didn't help either.

In some ways, she was right. Over the years, the meaning of "Intention" has morphed and strayed away from its original definition, which is "an aim that guides action." When we consider the word in this earlier usage, we can appreciate Intention as *purpose with a plan to get there.* As I walked her through this reasoning, she began to change her mind and came to see Intention as the perfect way to encapsulate her drive, her purpose, and her means to get there.

Most Westerners who have taken a yoga class or two may recall being asked to "set your intention" at the beginning of class. This is a form of Sankalpa, "a statement you can call upon to remind you of your true nature and guide your choices."[1] And it is more than just a nice focus for the practice session — it is a meditation on one's deepest desires and it can have a profound effect on one's life.

Scientists are beginning to see that the reason for this lies in our ability to train the brain. Recent findings in the burgeoning field of neuroplasticity outline our neurological capacity to change our beliefs, behaviors, and habits. Working with Intention is one way to do this.[2] Another is the simple act of practicing, such as when learning to play a musical instrument. Both scenarios require not just thinking about purpose but activating it.

In my personal and professional life, I have seen the powerful effect of using Intention to answer the why of communication. In my work I guide clients to create a Statement of Intention that becomes a focus for how they show up, act, and speak, even what words they choose. We then work on aligning their Intention with their Presence

---

1   McGonigal, Kelly. (2025 November 08). "How to Create a Sankalpa." *Yoga International*. https://yogainternational.com/article/view/how-to-create-a-sankalpa/
2   Weindling, Miranda. (2025 November 08). "The Science of Intention." *Uplift*. https://uplift.love/the-science-of-intention/

and their Story to create what I call Reverberation. One of my workshop participants described the experience this way: "The real aha moment was when we first practiced with the concept of Intention, where I could actually tell the difference in energy and engagement when I practiced that technique before a presentation than when I didn't."

In my workshops with clients, I carefully guide them through various exercises to help them discover and use Intention. My first lesson on the importance of Intention was far less deliberate and guided. I was in the middle of a stage performance for a play that was popular in theatrical circles at the time. The play was filled with emotional turns and touched on some fairly moving insights about relationships and life. All that is to say, the lines were important. Imagine my horror when I was on stage with just one other performer – e.g. all eyes were on us – and suddenly the lines I had practiced and thought I learned just weren't there. We were in the middle of a defining moment for the play, and I had completely lost my place. To make matters worse, it was one of the first times I had actual lines in a play – usually I sang, and songs, by the way, are much easier to memorize than spoken word. It's not that I was being lazy or negligent. I could recite my part in my sleep. I just couldn't do it at that very moment. It was like sleep paralysis, only instead of being in bed by myself, I was on stage with hundreds of people watching me.

At the time, I had yet to take an acting class, so I wasn't

aware that an actor prepares by doing more than just studying the overall story and lines. I soon discovered that an actor must also learn what motivates her character in every scene, her history, her backstory, and her relationship to everyone else. It is all intertwined. An actor must understand the Intention of the character they are portraying. This clear sense of Intention, or why the character does what she does on stage, helps keep the dialogue on point and enables the actors to intuitively make choices regarding gestures and movement. Without well-defined Intention, one can easily lose their place amidst the distractions of the audience and the bustle backstage.

And that's precisely what happened to me. Instead of seeing my lines as part of a complex interplay of relationships, motivations, and corresponding actions, they were simply words leading to a song. Without a clear Intention for delivering them, my lines lost real meaning, and I suddenly had no idea where I was in the scene nor how to continue. I stood dumbfounded and stricken until my scene partner rescued me with a couple of improvised remarks. Grateful, I came to my senses, jumped back into the dialogue, and went on. As we left the stage, my partner took my arm and whispered brusquely in my ear, "Don't ever look at me with those glazed eyes again!"

After that experience, I took a class on The Method. More commonly known as 'method acting,' The Method strives to internalize the process of acting by drawing on personal experiences to recreate emotions and responses. The basis for the technique is Russian theater practitioner Konstantin Stanislavski's system. Through this approach, actors create a more profound, more authentic performance. As I learned, different Intentions create different experiences. For instance, my Intention to learn lines as a lead-in to a song might have helped me get to the music faster (especially if I dropped a few lines), but it didn't help me find my place in the scene because the Intention was not related to the story.

Although I found it fascinating and helpful, the most thought-provoking part of the approach is what Stanislavski called the "super-objective," which is what a character wants from life more than anything throughout the film or play. The super-objective drives everything the character does on stage.

The difference between a character who has a super-objective and one who does not is evident to an audience because every human is at least somewhat clairvoyant. What I mean is the human brain can project into the mind of another person. It's what we do in the first 30 seconds of hearing a keynote speech to decide whether we should keep listening. It's what compels us to instantly trust a stranger or run the other way.

According to research, there is a specific part of the brain dedicated to mentalizing, a network that helps us predict behavior based on what we infer as another person's

Intentions.[3] Some people call this the "sixth sense" and consider it a "gift," but in reality, everyone tends to develop the skill as they mature. It's such an essential competence for social beings that we can't keep ourselves from judging others ...nor escape from being equally scrutinized.

Psychologists call this mentalizing The Theory of Mind. In short, we create theories about others' thoughts and Intentions which help us infer who others are.[4] With a dedicated neural network, we can get pretty good at it. We rely on experience to build those theories which is why it takes some maturity to put it all together. Over time we come to recognize when there are discrepancies in someone's words and action. As we get better at this, we may even notice contradictions in someone's tone of voice, their gestures, and their posture. We also notice when these are aligned. We usually express this as a sense of trust for someone, noting their authenticity, their genuineness.

Although scientists can only now show maps of the brain as people mentalize, the awareness of such brain activity is not new. In the 16th century, the artist Leonardo Da Vinci described the Theory of Mind from an artistic perspective in his notebook. "A good painter has two chief objects to paint, man and the intention of his soul; the former is easy, the

3   Krueger, Frank. Jorge Moll, Nikolaus Kriegeskorte, Roland Zahn, Maren Strenziok, Armin Heinecke, & Jordan Grafman. (2008). "Neural Correlates of Trust." *Proceedings of the National Academy of Sciences of the United States of America*. 104. 20084-9. 10.1073/pnas.0710103104.
4   Cherry, Kendra. (2025 November 08). "How the Theory of Mind Helps Us Understand Others." *VeryWellMind*. https://www.verywellmind.com/theory-of-mind-4176826

latter hard, because he has to represent it by the attitudes and movements of the limbs. The most important consideration in painting is that the movement of each figure expresses its mental state, such as desire, scorn, anger, pity, and the like."[5]

Just as we are unique personalities, our Theory of Mind is uniquely created through our personal experience. My own Theory of Mind often manifests as a distinct feeling that the person I am speaking with reminds me of someone else. One such experience went something like this: My husband and I were at the bar of a restaurant waiting for our table when he started a brief exchange with the couple next to us. We all traded small talk and introductions for a few minutes. As I was farthest away from them and the bar was noisy, I only caught a few words here and there. I watched as the others continued comparing notes on the wine we were all drinking. However, within a few minutes, I noticed how the woman's facial expressions seemed to belong on another face — she reminded me of someone.

This recognition, a key element in the formation of my Theory of Mind, sparked my curiosity. I studied and studied her, trying not to stare too much and racking my brain to remember who the other person was. Suddenly, it came to me. She reminded me of a friend. As I watched her interact with my husband, I sensed she was trying to be warm yet careful not to overstep — an inner tug-of-war I'd seen so often in my friend, which is what made the connection click. Once I

5   Isaacson, Walter. *Leonardo Da Vinci.* Simon & Schuster, 2017.

recognized that, I instantly attributed my friend's warmth and honesty to this woman and decided I wouldn't mind getting to know her.

One of the most important functions of mentalizing is determining whether we can trust others and one of the most fundamental determiners of trust is how well the words a person speaks correspond with the expressions, voice, and posture they present. As I described, I unconsciously use comparisons with the facial expressions of people I know to make those judgments. We intuitively — and very quickly — calculate volumes of data people unknowingly give off. Once we have innately assessed a person's Intention, similar to an online search, the congruity of the data will determine the degree to which we trust them. As you can imagine, this was immensely important before the days of Google.

Psychologists tell us we all make judgments based on people's faces, their body language, and their voices. With physical characteristics we are more likely to trust someone who looks like us and moves like us; with voices, we are more trusting of those who sound like us. In either case, we make those judgments within a staggering 100 milliseconds of first meeting someone.

To try this theory out, watch a television show with the sound muted. If you're like my daughter, you'll also need to turn off the subtitles! Watch people carefully. Observe their expressions, their gestures, their movements. Can you perceive their emotional state? Chances are you can. You may notice that the larger the emotions, the easier they are to discern. Take humor or anger, for instance. A tight-lipped scowl or wide-open smile speak volumes. But can you pick out more nuanced states of mind like jealousy, unease, or deception? Some people say they can.

When flying, instead of watching movies on his own screen, my husband likes to watch other people's movies — even though, and actually because, he can't hear the sound. He loves to see what he can figure out about the movie from the characters' expressions and behaviors. Then he watches the movie himself to see if he was right. He calls it an exercise in intuition; I call it an exercise in insanity. It is incredible, though, how much he picks up beyond emotional states. He can tell motives, plot structure, and even whole conversations!

So, how do we read Intention in others? Many believe that mastering the ability to do this is a key interpersonal skill that helps leaders lead, salespeople sell, and lawyers ... well, lawyer. Perhaps it's through micro expressions that we display Intention. Micro expressions are brief, involuntary facial movements. We all make them though we may not always be aware of them. Even blind people exhibit micro expressions in the same way as the sighted, indicating they are not learned from the environment.

The study of micro expressions was popularized by Dr. Paul Ekman, an American psychologist widely considered to be a pioneer in the study of emotions and their relation to facial expressions. [6] Micro expressions were also brought into the public eye by the popular U.S. television show, *Lie to Me*, which aired from 2009 to 2011. They have also been the subject of numerous pop psychology and culture articles.

Ekman described them as emotional leakage that exposes a person's true emotions. A quick internet search will yield a plethora of videos that capture micro-expressions in action, such as barely visible lip raises suggesting disgust, slightly upturned corners of mouths indicating happiness, and fast eye blinks demonstrating discomfort. One of the most comprehensive collections of high-res, slow motion videos capturing micro expressions is that of Kasia and Patryk Wezowski from The Center for Body Language in Belgium.[7]

If you're wondering if there are also macro expressions, the answer is yes. While micro expressions have a duration of less than 200 milliseconds, macro expressions last longer than 200 milliseconds. These are what people consider 'normal' facial expressions. Smiles and frowns, for instance, are macro expressions. Most individuals are quite apt at identifying and decoding these.[8]

Intuitively speaking, micro and macro expressions may indicate a person's unspoken Intention. However, just

---

6   Paul Ekman Group. (2025 November 08). "Paul Ekman: A Timeline of Achievements." *About Paul Eckman*. https://www.paulekman.com/about/paul-ekman/
7   Center for Body Language. (2025 November 08). https://centerforbodylanguage.com/
8   Shen, Xunbing, Qi Wu, Ke Zhao, & Xiaola Fu. (2025 November 08). "Electrophysiological Evidence Reveals Differences between the Recognition of Microexpressions and Macroexpressions." *Frontiers in Psychology*. https://www.frontiersin.org/journals/psychology/articles/10.3389/fpsyg.2016.01346

because we can accurately read macro and micro expressions some of the time, doesn't mean we can do it all the time. The truth is the interpretation of expressions does not always hold up under the rigor of the scientific method. In fact, many researchers have noted that felt emotions do not have a one-to-one correspondence to outward expressions.

There is a growing body of evidence that suggests that Micro Expression Theory is a source of mainstream entertainment but an unreliable means to determine intent, at least on its own.[9] It is disconcerting to know that Ekman's work has never been published, leading many scientists to challenge his claims. However, just because the study of micro and macro expressions is not the end-all decoder of intent does not mean that it is altogether wrong. This is a classic "yes, and" situation. *Yes*, expressions sometimes can be used to recognize underlying Intention, *and* they are more reliable when coupled with other cues.

One of the most important things we do with the impressions we pick up is to measure how much we trust someone. While trust is integral in our personal lives and how we relate to friends, families, and colleagues, it also plays a major factor in our decision-making process. For instance, we make major purchase decisions based on trust, such as cars and houses, or medical decisions, such as whether to get vaccinated. In fact, the more risk a scenario has, the more likely we are to rely on trust as a determiner of our course

9   Ibid.

of action. According to research in Germany, we decide on 'epistemic trustworthiness' — how much we trust knowledge from an expert — by assessing one's competence, adherence to scientific standards, and their perceived Intention. [10]

George Brooks, former Global Deputy, EY People Advisory Services, calls trust "the superpower that unleashes all others. It lays the foundation for responsible risk, which we've found can lead to more cohesive teams, greater resilience, and a strengthened bond with customers." According to Brooks, this happens through a leader's compassion, and their communication from the heart, reflecting vulnerability and a sense of purpose with which one agrees. [11]

It is easy to find validity in this world, but very difficult to find truth. While there is a growing need for trust within organizations, we can all start to build trust much closer to home where it matters most. One of the most important truths we need to discover to become an effective communicator is the truth of our own Intention.

Understanding our own Intention takes a high degree of self-awareness. Being honest with ourselves is not as easy or intuitive as it sounds. It's a simple fact that the more time we spend on this planet, the more decisions and actions we make. The more decisions and actions we make, the more consequences arise. It's an ever-expanding web of cause and

---

10   Hendriks F, Kienhues D, Bromme R (2015) "Measuring Laypeople's Trust in Experts in a Digital Age: The Muenster Epistemic Trustworthiness Inventory (METI)." *PLOS ONE* 10(10): e0139309. https://doi.org/10.1371/journal.pone.0139309
11   EY. "Unleashing Human Power to Do The Extraordinary." EYGM Limited, 2020.

effect. Every action of every individual interacts with the decisions and actions of other individuals — multiplied by eight billion people. In chaos theory this impossible calculus of probability is poetically expressed in the butterfly effect.

In the mid-twentieth century, mathematician and meteorologist Edward Lorenz was working with weather forecast models when he discovered that a tiny action, such as the flapping of a butterfly's wings, has progressive nonlinear knock-on effects which spread outward and across an inconceivable network of further changes, resulting in enormous and unpredictable effects such as a tornado weeks later on the other side of the planet.

Similarly, in this chaotic age of information (and misinformation and disinformation), many forces pull us in countless directions. From confirmation bias to anchoring to the hordes of algorithms used throughout the internet of things, we are caught in a web of heuristics which all conspire to influence us in ways we seldom even realize. Our Intentions are also part of that web and it all feeds into that network of cause and effect we mentioned. Our Intentions have consequences that are more far-reaching than we could ever imagine. That's not to say we need to paralyze ourselves thinking about our every Intention every minute of every day. It does suggest, however, that when it comes to important communication, the clearer we are about Intention, the more honest we are with ourselves, the more we can trust the consequence of that communication.

VOCALIZING AND HEARING INTENTION

Like most things in life, we should never rely on a single data point to prove a case. Similarly, we need a set of data, an array of evidence, to establish intent. One particularly rich vein of data is vocalization.

A person's vocal tone, inflection, and speech patterns give ample clues to their Intention. There may be hints to a person's emotional state, to their physical wellbeing, or even to their disposition toward a subject being discussed. In fact, a person's voice gives off so much personal information that the development of a vocal firewall may be more desirable than one would think. Studies have determined that besides emotions, a person's voice can give clues to their education, geographical location, family history, and occupation.

In the 1950s George L. Trager identified this phenomenon as 'paralanguage.' Later studies would show that paralanguage differs by culture and is learned.[12] It is also both conscious and unconscious and accompanies every vocal manifestation. It can be detected in sign language or lip reading. Simply put, you can't utter a sound without conveying some form of paralanguage.

Let's delve into emotions as an example. We often think of emotion as an ethereal, transitive force. Poets say it resides in the heart and is a matter of spirit; scientists say it resides in the brain and is more about chemicals than anything else.

---

12   Van Edwards, Vanessa. (2025 November 08). "Decoding Vocals – 21 Cues of Paralanguage & Prosody to Know." *Science of People*. https://www.scienceofpeople.com/paralanguage/

Personally, I believe emotions occur when the interconnected processes of interpretation, bodily reaction, and expression are activated in response to a situation, either external or internal.

While there is certainly a mental and even spiritual aspect to emotion, there is most obviously a physical aspect. We know this intuitively. Emotions in their physical manifestation erupt into laughter, cascade into tears, explode into anger. Since voice is also physical, it's no wonder that we can hear emotions.

Vocal sounds are made by using air we inhale through our nose or mouth and then exhale from our lungs. The air passes through our vocal folds and brings them together to vibrate. The sound resonates through bones and cavities in our bodies, is modulated by the muscles in our throats and mouths, then finally bursts forth into the world to be further shaped by the surfaces it bounces against.

As a species, humans distinguish themselves from non-primates with the ability to articulate faster and make a variety of sounds with a single breath. When it comes to expressing emotions vocally, changes in our muscles, breath, and brain affect our pitch, cadence, and inflection – in other words, our paralanguage. It is this paralanguage combined with the Theory of Mind that make it possible for us to pick up Intention in interpersonal communication.

I received a voicemail from my daughter recently. All she said was, "Hi, Mom. Call me." Four simple words conveying a simple request, but beyond the words so much more was communicated. I knew immediately something was wrong. It wasn't *what* she said, it was *how* she said it. Some people might call this intuition, but part of intuition is actually the human brain picking up on very real and natural cues.

Coupled with the ability for the voice to show emotion is the ability for the ear to pick up minute differences in the sound the voice produces. Humans can hear sounds between 20 Hz and 20 kHz and human speech produces frequencies on average between 100 to 1,000 Hz. The human ear can also perceive 1400 different pitches and 280 different levels of volume for each pitch it hears. Even tiny fluctuations in vocalizations can give away our emotional state.

The ability to hear changes in vocalization and attribute them to emotions is something we develop very early. A study done by researchers at the University of Geneva (UNIGE), in Switzerland showed that "babies have an early ability to transfer emotional information from the auditory mode to the visual."[13] Essentially, at a very early age we develop the ability to hear emotions. In fact, a 2019 study at UC Berkeley revealed that we can distinguish up to 24 emotions from brief vocalizations. Types of distinguishable emotions ranged from the predictable — 'triumph' and 'pain' — to the more nuanced sentiments like 'contentment' and 'realization.'[14] And if you are

---

13   Palama, Amaya. (2025 November 08). "Babies Make the Link between Vocal and Facial Emotion." Université de Genéve. https://www.unige.ch/communication/communiques/en/2018/les-bebes-relient-lemotion-dune-voix-a-celle-dun-visage/

14   Cowen, Alan, Hillary Elfenbein, Petri Laukka, & Dacher Keltner. (2018). "Mapping 24 Emotions Conveyed by Brief Human Vocalization." *American Psychologist*. 74. 698-712. 10.1037/amp0000399.

wondering just how brief those vocalizations can be before we pick up on emotional cues, the answer is one-tenth of a second. Vocalizations convey emotions faster than words.[15]

The human voice is an incredible broadcaster of emotion, second perhaps only to the ear's preternatural faculty to receive those sounds, and third to the brain's ability to decode all of the above. The bottom line is: If you feel an emotion, chances are no matter how hard you try to disguise it, someone will hear or even see it when you speak.

DEVELOPING INTENTION

Although it's important to be clear about Intention, we don't need to overthink it. Intentions don't need to be complex. In fact, the simpler the better. Some of the most successful brands in the world are known by one word. PayPal, Netflix, eBay, Nescafe, Facebook are all simple names that convey the spirit of their Intention.

In college, I worked at a small record shop. My boss was adamant that the name of the shop would indicate the nature of the business. In this case, it was The Turntable Records and Tapes. His Intention? To sell records and tapes. And yes, I am aware that today his store would be an antique store.

To determine Intention, we can think about the reasons to have a conversation, give a talk, or share a presentation.

15   Pell, M.D., Rothermich, K., Liu, P., Paulmann, S., Sethi, S., Rigoulot, S. "Preferential Decoding of Emotion from Human Non-Linguistic Vocalizations Versus Speech Prosody." *Biological Psychology*. Volume 111, 2015, Pages 14-25. ISSN 0301-0511. https://doi.org/10.1016/j.biopsycho.2015.08.008
(https://www.sciencedirect.com/science/article/pii/S0301051115300478)

Here is a sample list:

- To help the other person reach a decision
- To enlist others in a specific project
- To encourage others to buy a product
- To change a point of view
- To lead someone to act
- To request a sponsorship

The meeting or conversation associated with each bullet above might include the same attendees, but the Intention will determine the content as well as the environment in which each meeting takes place. For example, if the Intention is to help the other person reach a decision, it would be important to prepare by outlining the pros and cons of the situation. However, if the Intention is to change their point of view, we would need to prepare to be persuasive.

 **INSIGHT**

Robert Cialdini's Seven Principles of Persuasion make a handy checklist for narrowing down Intention.

- What gives me the authority to say this? (Credibility), and
- What am I willing to give them in exchange (Reciprocity)?
- How can I demonstrate my commitment (Consistency)?
- What will be missing if we don't do this? (Scarcity)
- How can I demonstrate that I care? (Likeability)
- Where have I seen this before? (Social Proof)
- How will I show that we are in this together? (Unity)

https://www.influenceatwork.com/

AUTHENTICATING INTENTION

She spoke five languages, was undeniably bright, and had climbed the corporate ladder to become a highly successful VP of sales for a large corporation. With all she had on her plate, she would not have been in the workshop if it weren't for her team insisting that she join them. I was impressed with how she presented herself, her intelligence and sense of humor, and her stories of living all over the world.

Her team was a group of equally brilliant high-achievers, and we had a great time exploring the components of communicating with impact. They tried out new skills and laughed at habits that can knock the punch out of an otherwise effective communicator.

As we moved through the day, people opened more and more, increasing their honesty with each other and with themselves until, when we wrapped up, we all felt a warm glow of camaraderie that caused us to pause and sit in silence just for a minute. It was then that their very cosmopolitan leader leaned into the others around the table and said, "Today, my biggest takeaway is that if we're true to our core and to the authenticity of that Intention, then the conversation can only flow from a place of trust and confidence."

Years later, we reminisced over that beautiful day, and she said, "I never forgot the power of authentic Intention. I used it to get my promotion. It was amazing because, I said: 'Here's my Intention in this company, and in the world,' and because I had to stick to my conviction of this Intention, I was able to ask for what I wanted." And she got it.

When stepping in front of an audience, large or small, or settling in to have an important conversation, virtually or physically, we will be most successful if we first determine what we are trying to accomplish. In the journey to align vocalizations and expressions with Intention, authentic Intention is critical. There's no getting around it — we have to be honest with ourselves to show up with impact to others. When we're honest with ourselves about our Intention and when we allow that honesty to flow through to our audience, we can achieve something truly golden — authenticity.[16]

An Operations VP I knew was exceptionally good at aligning his outward expressions with his inward Intention, but he did so unknowingly. Every quarter his business would hold a town hall meeting, and he was expected to give an update on operations. This often included making an appeal to the audience to get behind a difficult project or step-up performance to deliver challenging targets.

When he was on stage you could almost see him physically struggling to stay on script. The audience would wait in anticipation for the moment when he would drop all pretense and just say what was on his mind. It would often start with something like: "Listen folks, I gotta be straight with you... [hammer drop]" or "I can't remember everything they told me to say, but here's what you gotta know... [hammer

16   Peters, Kate. (2018 September 25). "Let's Be Real: Authenticity, Presence & Intention." Vocal Impact. https://www.vocalimpact.net/2018/09/25/lets-be-real-authenticity-presence-and-intention/

drop]." He would couple his words with gestures like throwing up his hands or shaking his head in exasperation. He would then speak in his own words according to what he believed in his heart.

And the audience would listen. He spoke from his one true Intention: to be honest with his audience, to be direct, to be himself. When he did this, the audience trusted him. Whether they agreed with him or not, they trusted him. This is the power of clear, authentic Intention.

This VP understood what he needed to say — his own truth and not a canned speech from the communications team. He knew his targets, he knew the challenges, he knew the business rationale. This, after all, was his job and had been for a very long time. He also knew what his people needed to hear. He knew they had no patience for complex stories or multi-layered strategies. They wanted the plain truth even if it was difficult to hear. Strategy and theories could come from the CFO and Marketing VP, but the tangible, authentic truth needed to come from him, the operations guy.

When determining Intention, our first job is to clearly determine what we want the audience or conversation partner to do. What is the call to action? On a much smaller scale, the basic philosophy is the "future-back" approach that visionaries such as Steve Jobs and Jeff Bezos have used to create innovative companies. In context of communication and Intention, we can look ahead at what we want our conversation partner to take away from the conversation.

Knowing how the interchange must end, we can more easily plan back to how we are going to get there which will help determine Intention.

CALIBRATING INTENTION

It is critical to know what an audience wants to hear, to know what makes them tick, what keeps them up at night, what motivates them. Most importantly, what is their disposition toward the message you want to deliver. Are they in agreement with your position? Are they willing participants in whatever it is that is being offered? Do they disagree? Are they skeptical?

Developing Intention is more multi-layered than linear. The audience's disposition toward my Intention will help shape that Intention. It is recursive. If a presenter wants to sell her audience on an idea, but knows that they are adamantly against that idea, her Intention may become to soften their stance. To uncover Intention, we must take measures to understand the audience.

An historian was asked to give a speech to a local chapter of a conservative American organization. His Intention was to speak as someone who could teach them something new about a piece of American history. As an expert on President Lincoln, he prepared a talk that gave fresh insight into Lincoln's character. In addition, he thought it would be fun to weave in some common questions about Lincoln that were asked online. As he looked out at the sea of gray hair before him, he was pleased to see them smiling and agreeable. However, one of the questions was, "Did Lincoln have syphilis?" When he posed that question, he encountered a noticeable shift in the room and a considerable amount of throat-clearing.

Immediately realizing the mistake of bringing the topic of venereal disease to such an elderly, conservative group, he tried to gloss over it. He even feigned surprise at finding the word in his notes. But after what seemed like a lifetime of awkwardness, he felt a need to simply move on. So, he changed the subject to Lincoln's considerable sense of humor and quoted one of Lincoln's jokes, "How many legs does a dog have if you call his tail a leg?" The answer? "Four. Saying that a tail is a leg doesn't make it a leg."

Although the talk was met by polite applause, there were those who refused to clap, and the historian regretted that he misjudged the audience. It was a good lesson to learn. A few days later, he gave a talk to a different crowd, but he knew them far better. He recounted the story of his faux pas with a lot of confidence and some regret. They thought it was hilarious.

There's just no way we can know, much less meet, every expectation of every individual person we will be addressing, but we can easily work out what an audience generally thinks and feels, and that will reveal some basic truths. The research into an audience is similar to what communications professionals do by conducting a stakeholder analysis. This analysis maps out the sentiments and dispositions of the anticipated audiences and key influencers. Now, while the average person may lack the expertise and time required for such an exercise, you'd be surprised how close some thoughtful reflection will get to the goal. The more familiar we are with an audience, be it an individual or an auditorium filled with individuals, the easier this will be.

TAPPING INTO EMPATHY

In assessing an audience's disposition, one tool that virtually everyone has in their toolkit is empathy. Empathy plays a large role in understanding an audience. The term "empathy" is over a hundred years old and has been practiced since humankind could first think and feel. Despite this and the fact that it's been a hot topic in psychology and neuroscience for many years, a definitive clinical definition has proven problematic. In general terms, though, we can describe it as "the capacity to understand or feel what another person is experiencing from within their frame of reference, that is, the capacity to place oneself in another's position."[17]

Researchers generally agree on two broad categories of empathy – cognitive and emotional – and recent studies point to a deep interdependence between the two. Cognitive empathy is about understanding someone else's perspective.[18] It involves taking in their context, their situation, and

---

17   Wikipedia. (2025 November 08). "Empathy." *Wikipedia*. https://en.wikipedia.org/wiki/Empathy

18   Pessoa, Luiz. (2009). "Cognition and Emotion." *Scholarpedia*, 4(1):4567. http://www.scholarpedia.org/article/Cognition_and_emotion

imagining how they might think about a particular subject. Emotional empathy is feeling what another feels, essentially putting yourself in "someone else's shoes." Some people describe it as "compassion."

A friend of mine is a consultant in a large accounting firm and operates on a global scale. His work involves collaborating with clients and colleagues on multicultural projects. One day, as we were about to have coffee, his phone rang, and he said, "I have to take this call. There is a problem with our project in India." I sipped my coffee and waited for him to take the call outside. I could see through the window that the situation was tense. As I waited, I reflected on what I knew of his role. He had been asked to step in and create his organization about ten years earlier and had grown the business from nothing to a well-oiled, high performing machine. I also reflected on what I knew of the man who had developed the ability to evaluate multiple conflicting viewpoints, sort through the possibilities and find solutions for all involved when others might have given up.

When he returned, he seemed much less tense. I guess the problem had been solved. When I suggested as much, he stirred his coffee and then said thoughtfully, "The biggest problem is that everyone wants something different." He shrugged his shoulders and continued, "I'm not an expert in other cultures, but I know people, and things get mired down when people don't feel heard." He went on to explain that it's not that you have to please everyone, but the real job is to understand each perspective and make sure they at least feel considered.

"That takes time," he pointed out, "and most people are not willing to do it. But, frankly, the value of staying out of the power play tug-of-war and being willing to listen is that we get productivity. That's how we win over and over again."

By practicing empathy, we can glimpse outside of our individual silos and understand what matters to our listeners. This is important because we are all motivated by different factors, care about different issues, and are persuaded by different ideas.

It doesn't take training or being a gifted psychologist to practice empathy, we just have to be decent human beings. Also, like most things in life, the more we practice empathy the better we get at it. And the better we get at it, the better our skills as a communicator, a leader, and an all-around good human being will become. In terms of communicating with audiences both large and small, the better we become at practicing empathy, the better we become with "reading the room."

The next time you need to give a presentation or have a conversation, take inventory of what's going on in the minds and hearts of your listeners. Think about where they might be cognitively as well as emotionally, then do the same for yourself. What do you think and feel about the topic you'll be addressing as well as the context from which you will be doing it? Does the topic make you anxious, angry, happy, enthused? Consider the similarities between your position toward the topic and the position of your audience toward it. Perhaps more importantly, consider the differences. In your communications you will be linking commonalities and bridging gaps.

If you are excited about a topic but you know your audience is dreading it, think about why that is. Maybe you know something about the topic that your audience doesn't. Your Intention, then, may be to persuade them to a different perspective by educating them or revealing key information.

 **INSIGHT**

How to practice empathy for better communication

- Initiate conversations.
- Ask open-ended questions.
- Talk less listen more.
- Imagine how you would feel if you were they.
- Avoid assumptions and suspend judgment.

SHIFTING INTENTIONS

I have been asked if Intentions ever shift. The obvious answer is that over time, of course, Intentions may shift as circumstances and various dynamics shift. But can Intentions shift in the short-term, say for instance, during a presentation or meeting? And if so, how can you manage that shift so that everything doesn't fall apart?

I live in California and have for quite some time. For better or worse, it's my home. One of the toughest things to get used to — besides the wildfires, politics, and smog — is the earthquakes. Oh, and the traffic, but for now let's talk about earthquakes. One of the most memorable was the Sylmar quake in 1971. It struck at 6 a.m. with a magnitude of 6.6, a forceful jolt that I felt even though I was 45 miles away from the epicenter. In fact, the shock was felt for 300 miles along the southern California coastal region and as far inland as Las Vegas, Nevada. My sister, who was much closer to the epicenter, had a particularly close call. She opened her eyes just in time to see a plate that had popped off the wall above her in the quake tumbling toward her head. She quickly reached up and caught it and lived to tell the story, thank God.

Intention can be like earthquakes — it can shift underneath us without warning. This shift can occur during the process of preparing communication and trying to identify the Intention. It can also occur when participants don't agree with the Intention for a meeting or a conversation.

It's likely that every businessperson reading this has been in a meeting where the Intention shifted. For example, perhaps the reason for assembling was to track the status of a project, but someone in the meeting started talking about a completely different project. The shift pulled the meeting "into the weeds."

The good news is, unlike earthquakes, there is a way of controlling the damage created by such a shift. By stating the

Intention at the top of the meeting, meetings can more easily be kept on topic. In addition, meetings and conversations are much more productive if everyone involved agrees on the Intention.

Of course, we still have to be watchful for shifts which deviate from the meeting's Intention. Again, the key here is listening. Listening is different than hearing. While most of us worry about expressing ourselves effectively and getting our ideas across with impact, focusing on real listening is critical for great communication. Listening is key in first establishing the meeting's Intention. It is also critical in identifying if and when the meeting has shifted off topic.

In an article in *Psychology Today*, psychologist Sherrie Bourg Carter reminds us "the best listeners recognize that they cannot succeed without seeking out information from those around them and they let those people know that they have unique input that is valuable."[19] There is no better way to know an audience than by listening to them. By listening to them, we invite them to become a partner, to enter into dialogue, to achieve a common goal.

ACTIVATING INTENTION

We don't have to wait to give a presentation to put our Intention into action. The reality is we communicate every day in a wide variety of situations. From casual conversations to

---

19   Carter, Sherrie Bourg. (2025 November 08). "The Art and Value of Good Listening." *Psychology Today*. https://www.psychologytoday.com/us/blog/high-octane-women/201209/the-art-and-value-of-good-listening?collection=107271

interpersonal exchanges to formal discussions, in a single day we may have dozens of opportunities to apply Intention. And it doesn't have to be in person. In today's world we can easily spend more time on the phone and in video conferences than we do in face-to-face scenarios.

Many people think conversation is dead, but I'm not convinced. In fact, I'm optimistic it is having a comeback. With that in mind, it may be a time for a refresher on how to have intentional, meaningful conversations as opposed to sporadic, superficial chats. Not that those chats aren't needed — they are part of our daily rituals and help ease many social situations.

Conversations, dialogue, or discussion, unlike light chatter, require some degree of planning. We're not talking Gantt charts or complicated spreadsheets, but some

 **EXERCISE**

- **Step one:** Decide what you want to accomplish. What do you want to get out of the conversation? Be honest with yourself.

- **Step two:** Think about how your audience may react and what you want them to do. What is their disposition toward the topic? Are they pro, con, indifferent? Remember to use your empathy. (The answers to Step one and Step two define your Intention.)

- **Step three:** Be prepared to share your Intention and, if appropriate to the situation, take time to ask them what they hope to accomplish during the discussion.

- **Step four:** Have the discussion.

deliberate forethought. Whether we commit our thoughts to writing or mentally review them is a personal choice. A general rule of thumb, though, is the more complicated the message, the better it is to document.

Now, planning to have a conversation and then actually having it go the way it was planned are two different things. The problem is, there is at least one other person in an exchange and while we can do a lot to understand their perspective, they have complete control over how they react. The truth is conversations can go in any direction at any time. That lack of control can be scary, which is why a clear Intention is a good way to begin.

CREATING A STATEMENT OF INTENTION

We have been thinking about Intention as something that drives a communications action. Intention, however, is much grander than the driving force for a presentation or conversation. Intentions can be larger than life. We all have an Intention for our lives whether we are aware of it or not. Having this grander Intention gives us an overarching guide that influences all the other smaller Intentions. That's why I developed a way to discover your own.

I started working with Statements of Intention (SOI) many years ago. I was a participant in a workshop focused on finding a North Star for one's work, and the facilitator introduced the idea of creating a statement that could be used as a guide for my choices. It was fun and clarifying, so I began working on one I could use to help clients move closer to the way they intend to show up.

Over time, I developed four questions; the first three questions seek to discern who we are as our best self, what we enjoy most in our work, and how we want to interact with others. The final question is about the vision that motivates us, something so much bigger than ourselves that it is mostly aspirational, but also something we would love to be part of. The answers to the four questions go into a template which we then shape into a Statement of Intention.

What's wonderful is how magical the statements feel to the participants. We've heard comments like "Wow, this is exactly what I want my life to be!"; "It's a spectacular exercise. That's why I have a big old smile on my face"; and "I can't believe how it came together to perfectly describe my best self." When we ask, "If you showed up as this person the next time you have a meeting with your staff, your boss, or your organization, would it change the conversation?" The answer is most often, "Yes!"

Some people find their personal Intention difficult to figure out, even with the template. Once they get comfortable with it, however, sensing it is valid and authentic even if just for today, the neuroplasticity of the brain helps us make the choices and changes needed to be the person in the statement. When there is clarity about a life Intention, all the other smaller Intentions — the ones for presentations, conversations, speeches — are easier to find.

One interesting aspect I've noticed about the grander Intention is that senior leaders almost always have one before we start working together even if they don't call it by the same name.

If you have a life Intention, should you also have a work Intention? Considering the now decades-old debate about work/life balance, some people say that work and life are two distinct things; others point to the fact that work feels more like home and home like work. Modern workplaces have gyms, coffee shops, banks, and much, much more. Depending on where we are in the world, our workplace may even have places of worship.

When we think about the home, more homes than ever have fully equipped offices with multiple monitors and high-speed internet. With the 2020 pandemic, these home offices became a lifeline for people to keep working and for businesses to stay operational. They became the de facto business continuity plan.

The reality is the idea of work/life balance is a quaint notion of yesteryear. Work and life are fluid and mostly indistinguishable. All that is to say, if we can create a life statement that also encompasses our work, fantastic. At one time we were taught this was something to avoid, but in fact it may be entirely natural. If we feel we need separate ones, that's okay too.

A personal SOI should be a brief reminder of what we do and why we do it. It's good practice to keep the statement in a notebook, phone memo, laptop, and on the desk – places where it's visible throughout the day to help prepare talks, sales pitches, or discussions. I keep mine in a frame by my desk. Spending two or three minutes every morning consciously reviewing it and thinking about how it applies to

 **EXERCISE:**

Get out a sheet of paper and prepare to write, OR open a blank digital document. Write the answers to these four questions.

1. What are your top 3 strengths (write as adjectives i.e. intelligent, happy, strong, etc.)?
2. What part of your work is most important to you?
3. What are 3 verbs that describe how you want to interact with others (i.e. guide, direct, inspire, etc.?
4. What is your vision for your life? (Something hard to attain that will inspire and motivate you (i.e. world peace, a sustainable future, a kind city)

Now use the answer to fill in the blanks below.
My intention is to be a (top 3 strengths) _____, _____, and _____ leader, who is focused on (goal for work)_____. I _____(3 verbs about interaction with others), _____, and _____ others in order to bring into reality my vision of (vision)_____.

The result is the first draft of your Statement of Intention. Work with it until it feels right. You can change it anytime. Then write it down and keep a copy of it where you can see it every day. Use it to guide how you show up and what you say in meetings, emails, and presentations. Ask yourself, if I show up as this person will it change the conversation I am planning?

the day ahead is useful. At the end of the day, it's helpful to spend a couple minutes reviewing how Intention played out — did the day go as intended and, if not, what can be learned?

I know a remarkable technologist who begins her day by rising early, taking her dog for a walk, and then settling down with her calendar. We share a close friendship and often enjoy virtual coffee during this time. While she has been a supportive listener and witness to the growth of my business and philosophy, our career paths differ greatly — hers often shrouded in secrecy or beyond my understanding; mine involving other people and at times, very public.

One Monday, I called her and although she answered, she mentioned she was in a rush. The upcoming week was packed, and she needed to finalize her Intention calendar before a business call in about 20 minutes. Intention calendar? Naturally, I was intrigued. When I asked her about it, she explained that she had started experimenting with Intention after I sent her instructions for creating a personal Statement of Intention. She found it so interesting that she began crafting Intention statements for her upcoming meetings on Monday mornings, focusing on the most crucial ones and using her personal statement as a guide. It has now become an integral part of her routine, streamlining her planning, aiding in the creation of presentations, and facilitating focused discussions. She thanked me and had to rush off, saying, "My Intention is waiting." And obviously, she has become not only a friend but also my favorite student!

If you want to create a personal SOI, the steps are outlined in the box above. Remember, we don't always create the perfect statement the first time. The SOI may need adjusting here and there and it may need more adjustment as we implement it. If so, that's okay. More often than not, though, it is our behavior that needs adjustment to fit the statement, and not the statement that needs to be adjusted to fit an ever-shifting range of behaviors. An Intention statement is meant to keep us on track and true to ourselves.

We may find ourselves struggling to stay aligned with our statement, but we can observe and take notes on what happened and how we might do things differently the next time. If we find we're staying on track, great. If we need adjustment, we can tighten our Intention or create a more

 **EXERCISE**

- **Step one:** Sit down with your calendar on Sunday evening or Monday morning.
- **Step two:** Look ahead at your week. What important meetings and conversations are scheduled?
- **Step three:** Create an Intention for each one by asking what do I want to accomplish and how will I get us there? Write the answers down in the calendar, or in a separate document.
- **Step four:** Use the statements of Intention to plan what you will do and say for each meeting or conversation.
- **Step five:** Refer to your Intention statements before, during and after each event.

aspirational and challenging statement. The trick, of course, is knowing when to stop. It is easy to revise a good draft into extinction.

FROM VISION TO REALITY

In 2010, hearing a city official talk about kindness in government was rare. However, the newly elected mayor of a large California city ran a family business and had served on the city council for many years. He became mayor because he wanted to make a difference in the city, and he had a crazy idea. The idea came to him from a holistic doctor whose young daughter, was tragically killed in an auto accident. She had written beautiful words on kindness during her short life. This inspired her father to spread the kindness message. He said "in medicine you can treat the symptoms, or you can holistically treat the body to heal from within. That is what I do as a holistic doctor." He then said..."I think the same principle applies to a city. You can either treat the symptoms, or you can stimulate the city to heal from within...and I think that has something to do with kindness ." That was the lightbulb moment for Tom. He knew it was true. So, he developed an Intention for his work as mayor that was both aspirational and challenging – Create a city of kindness and freedom.

Once he was clear about his Intention, the mayor started telling stories about kindness and freedom. Every talk ended with a clear statement of his belief that kindness and freedom matter. He spoke with passion. At first, people were skeptical, even critical, and mocked. However, his Intention was unwavering, and things began to happen.

Although there are many ways in which this approach could be manifested, my favorite story involved the children in the community. The mayor worked with the school district to create a program where children would log a million acts of kindness in a year. Over 25,000 K through 6 kids participated, which changed the schools. One principal at the toughest school said the calls to the principal for bullying were cut in half. District-wide, suspensions were cut in half.

This is what I love about Intention – it not only aids in creating rich, unambiguous communication but also facilitates making a vision a reality. Just as the mayor's Intention as the leader of the city made his vision a reality, individual Intention can shape how we show up, making our vision of ourselves a reality.

The practice of using Intention to guide our behavior is just that – a practice, which is the application of an idea, belief, or method, as opposed to a theory relating to it. In other words, Intention is powerful because it is more than a theory. It is purpose with a plan. Once clear, it takes our dedication to consciously apply Intention to shape our behavior, our choices, what we say and how we say it, but the result is communication with the kind of impact that brings visions to life.

REFLECTION
THE POWER OF INTENTION

When I think about the power that Intention can have, I think about the power of a simple phrase — Thank you. A friend observed a conversation between my partner and me wherein we said "thanks" to each other a dozen times. Afterward, she said, "That seems like a lot of work." In our family, we practice saying thanks. It's a ritual for us; it expresses gratitude and that we take nothing for granted because we came together after our respective divorces and raised a Brady Bunch with all its complexities. Because it wasn't always that way. But today, we feel it, mean it, and say it…often.

Sometimes, "Thanks" is just another pretty word. It's worth considering that, according to *Webster*, being "thankful" is to be conscious of a benefit received. However, saying "thanks" is just an informal, polite expression of gratitude. In other words, we can say "thanks," but if we don't really feel thankful or are not really conscious of the benefit received, our expression of gratitude falls flat. Being polite is often an empty act, one without clear Intention. However, if we ensure that what we say reflects the reason we are using those words and the way we say them, the act of saying 'thank you' is far from empty, it is filled with authentic gratitude.

We defined Intention earlier as purpose with a plan or the aim that guides action. Thinking of the aim when expressing gratitude, the result of using words of appreciation to someone should be that they feel appreciated. Again, the words fall flat when the Intention is to say the words just because it's the right thing to do.

Non-profits depend upon the kindness and generosity of those who have the resources to support them. As an advocate and supporter of the arts and education I've received plaques, photos, awards, and other accolades in recognition of and gratitude for my support. However, many of them felt empty because it was clear the Intention was to either "do the right thing" by the donors or keep the funds coming. I am sure that when a non-profit leadership team really stops to consider how dependent they are on donors for their existence the plaque has more impact.

So how can we find that alignment when "thank you" is appropriate but we are not feeling it? If we say it anyway people will pick up the Intention of being appropriate and the thank you will lose its impact. But if we take a moment to get clear about why "thank you" is appropriate, we will be more intentional in a way that will be reflected in those words and perhaps even in how we say them and the Intention to show gratitude will be clear.

CHAPTER 2

THE SECOND PRINCIPLE, **STORY**

I ka nānā nō a ʻike:
by observing, one learns
I ka hoʻolohe nō a hoʻomaopopo:
by listening one attains understanding

– ʻŌlelo Noʻeau, Hawaiian Proverbs from Oral Traditions

 **WHAT YOU WILL LEARN**

CHAPTER 2: STORY

The brain's language — and the bridge between minds.

What You'll Learn

- Why stories are the brain's preferred way to process meaning.
- The difference between stories and "Story."
- How to craft authentic Story that reflects your values.
- Where to find compelling personal or professional stories.
- Listening as a Story skill.

Key Takeaways

- Story is content that connects, is memorable, and inspires.
- Story brings your Intention to life and makes it memorable.
- Storytelling is not performance — it's an act of relationship.
- Your voice becomes magnetic when your Story is true and Intentional.

UNDERSTANDING STORY

I love Hawaii and have had the good fortune to travel there often. When visiting Hawaii, it's easy to get caught up in tourist traps, hitting the expected attractions featured in the media – the beaches, the restaurants, the stunning natural landmarks, and historical sites. These aren't bad things – they're popular for a reason – but the true gems of the islands lie off the beaten paths and far from the madding crowd.

From my experience, that's how most things in life are – you have to move beyond popular expectations before you can see things for what they truly are. We must read a book, see a movie, hear a song more than once before it starts to yield itself. That's how it is with Hawaii. When travelers spend time in the local areas getting to know more about the people, the land, and the history, the real beauty of Hawaii begins to emerge.

One of the special treasures I've discovered in Hawaii lies in the very simple custom of "talking story." "Let's talk story" is an invitation you might hear often while there. It's a great oral tradition of sharing history, ideas, opinions, and the events of the day with other people. My husband is from Hawaii and so has a lot of family there. On one of my first visits to the islands, I met his favorite uncle who came to our hotel to meet me and talk story. I looked forward to an evening of storytelling where I'd learn more about the family. At the time, I didn't know what "talking story" meant.

After dinner, we met in the hotel lobby and walked

outside through lush, tropical foliage scented with ginger and plumeria, winding through the hotel grounds until we reached a *lanai* out by the pool. We settled into comfortable chairs to watch the sunset, and the two began conversing. They asked questions like "How've you been?" and "What have you been up to?"

The two traded pleasantries a little awkwardly, trying to catch up on the years between this time and the last visit to Maui. I was also invited to join in, but I felt more comfortable as an observer. After all, my Intention was to learn more about my husband and his family.

As I waited for the storytelling to begin, I noticed that Uncle often created space in the conversation and said nothing, letting the sounds around us — the birds, the water, the insects — be part of our personal environment. After a period of silence, the anecdotes and laughter would flow again. There was humor, there were emotions, but most of all there was a sense of being present in the conversation, being in the moment. I heard references to my husband's childhood, but we also did a lot of sitting quietly, looking out at the ocean as it faded from blue to grey.

It felt odd then, a conversation so punctuated by silence but also so real and natural. This type of communication was a stark contrast to the fast-paced, information-driven conversations I was used to in my daily life. I thought there must be something I was missing or that I was supposed to do. But it also felt good. Something about taking the time to be genuinely present without looking at a watch or an agenda was nice.

After a couple of hours, Uncle stood, gave us both hugs, and we walked him back up the meandering path to the lobby where he got into his car and left.

I turned to my husband and said, "I thought we were going to hear a lot of your uncle's stories."

"Why did you think that?" he asked.

"You said we were going to talk story with him."

He laughed and said, "That's just what we call visiting with each other."

I took him at his word but reflected on it later. It wasn't just a visit. I knew that and he knew that, but he didn't want to cheapen it by calling too much attention to it. It was a time for sharing what has heart and meaning, for being connected in multiple ways. I've never forgotten that experience.

Rosa Say is a workplace aloha coach and author of the book, *Managing with Aloha: Bringing Hawai'i's Universal Values to the Art of Business.*[20] She told me this about the tradition of talking story: "I think of it as a relationship starter which goes a bit beyond small talk, with the assumption that you want to connect with a person's Aloha Spirit, and so more personal inquiry is okay, and even expected. We often say there is no deal making in business unless a relationship of some kind exists first, and talking story with someone with

---

20　Say, Rosa. *Managing with Aloha: Bringing Hawai'i's Universal Values to the Art of Business.* Ho'ohana Publishing, 2016.

no transactional expectations, just connection, is the way to start."

Although I was a bit confused that evening on Maui, over the years I've come to understand that unstructured and open communication, whether we tell actual stories or not, is important because even in casual conversation we take chances. If we leave space for anyone to say anything, much as we do in improv theater, that vulnerability invites relationship.

Similarly, through the act of telling stories and in the act of hearing stories, we share a bit of our humanity. It is in how we tell the story, how we express the events and our thoughts that surround them. It is in the words we use and the feelings, or lack thereof, that we demonstrate Intention. Equally, in hearing a story our empathy is with the person who is telling it to us, it is in our own reactions to them as a storyteller and the story itself. When you take both of these factors in — the telling and the hearing — it is the act of sharing that builds the relationship. As one of my clients told me, "Relationships first, business second."

STORY WITH A CAPITAL 'S'

Talking story is an example of what I call Story with a capital 'S' as opposed to story with a lowercase 's.'

Definition: Story with a capital S is a vital communication component which is critical to impact. It is not just "content" because it extends further than just words and media. Story with a capital S is content that connects. It connects because it shares common experience, stirs our emotions, and lights up our imaginations.

So, what kind of content can be defined as Story? Stories with a narrative arc, as we shall see, are engineered to have these types of effects, but Story with a capital S doesn't always have to be so conspicuous. Phatic communication, or small talk, that reveals a bit about the speaker can also be Story. So can expressive words, humor, emotions, and evocative statements; demonstrated vulnerability and open and interactive communication can be Story — all of which may lead to deeper engagement with others which has the happy benefit of increasing our impact.

Sometimes, we can better understand a concept if we know what it is not. In the case of Story, it is not a presentation that dives into the topic without introducing the speaker or acknowledging the audience. It is not a flat, monotonous delivery, or avoidance of emotion. It's not a timeline of events, an exposition, or an argument, nor is it a progress report. Story is not a graph, chart, or spreadsheet that fails to acknowledge the human experience behind every cell. None of these examples are Story because they lack connection.

Humans crave connection. This truth became painfully evident during the pandemic of 2020 when 67% of the world was forced to self-isolate to stop the spread of COVID-19.[21] A survey of people who were isolated revealed a high correlation between social isolation and lower levels of well-being and satisfaction with lifestyles. At its worst this creates greater instances of anxiety, depression, and even suicide. As much as we might complain about our fellow human beings at times, people need people. In fact, we've learned that in humans the single best predictor of physical health and well-being, as well as future longevity, is the number and quality of close friendships.[22]

I am not suggesting that to have impact you must have a personal connection with everyone in the audience, but I am saying that knowing your audience, being vulnerable with them, and understanding what matters to them is more important than ever. This is where connection begins. Leaders who are open about themselves are more likely to be perceived as trustworthy and credible by others, and worthy of a deeper relationship.

When businesses sent everyone home to work in 2020, it was a time of great uncertainty. No one knew how long it was going to last, how many facets of daily life were going to be affected, and whether or not the businesses themselves would remain solvent. One of my clients at the time, Pascal,

21 Clair, R. , M. Gordon, M. Kroon, et al. "The Effects of Social Isolation on Well-Being and Life Satisfaction During Pandemic." *Humanit Soc Sci Commun* 8, 28 (2021). https://www.nature.com/articles/s41599-021-00710-3
22 Yang, Y.C., C. Boen, K. Gerken, T. Li, K. Schorpp, & K.M. Harris. "Social Relationships and Physiological Determinants of Longevity across the Human Life Span." *Proceedings of the National Academy of Sciences. U.S.A.* 113 (3) 578-583, https://doi.org/10.1073/pnas.1511085112 (2016).

was an executive in a large corporation. He was successful because of his business acumen and ability to solve complex problems. In spite of the trend toward storytelling in business, he resisted sharing stories in his presentations and formal interactions, believing that it detracted from getting down to business. His perspective changed in March 2020 when offices closed due to COVID-19, and the pandemic lingered.

Pascal began to hear about people working from home while also managing their children's schooling, and others with family members who were critically ill. He learned of a team member who was anxious because his wife, a frontline worker at a hospital, had not been home in over a week. Another colleague had a daughter stranded in Europe, unable to return home.

During that time, even with the increasing popularity of meeting on video platforms, Pascal kept in touch with his broader organization through a series of blog posts. Mostly, they were the standard corporate messages about uncertainty and resilience. Yet, at heart he was much more concerned about the humans in his organization than he often let on, and he began to think of writing something else, something more personal such as how he was feeling about the isolation. He set to work.

Later that day, while working on his blog, he heard a loud commotion outside. He looked out the window and saw a long line of cars adorned with streamers and signs reading, "Happy

Birthday, José." Just then, he saw a little boy and his parents run out from the house across the street, shouting and waving excitedly. Due to the cancellation of physical birthday parties, the parents of children from José's classroom had brought his classmates to his home to celebrate his birthday, albeit from a distance. Pascal laughed with delight. He began to see the moment as lighter and more hopeful, adapted his post about isolation and began to write about what he experienced and the joy he felt seeing it. He finished his post that evening and sent it in to be published.

The next morning after coffee he turned on his computer and was shocked. Previously, he had received only a few comments on his posts, but this time he garnered over 290 comments and thousands of views. People shared their own stories and expressed gratitude for his authenticity. Some shared funny stories, some poignant. But regardless of what they wrote, Pascal could see that he had connected with people on his team in a very different way. By exposing his vulnerability, Pascal transcended mere storytelling and achieved a deeper narrative. By sharing his struggles, he created a space for others to do the same, fostering a sense of community and understanding during those challenging times. It was a turning point that changed his mind about the importance of Story.

Just as in written communication, getting to Story should be the goal when speaking at a meeting or a conference, but Story is different for each audience. Not everyone can relate to stories about birthday parties when they want to hear from an esteemed expert on their favorite topic. Years ago, when I attended my first main-stage conference keynote, I was intrigued to be initiated into the world of business presentations. In the end, however, I left the room perplexed. In front of me was a stage with lighting and a backdrop just like the stages on which I'd performed. The production values were so high that it felt more like a rock concert than a business event. Three huge screens flanked the rear of the stage, and several high-tech monitors peeked up in front with a large crew managing both the stage and technology. Music blasted and thumped as almost 2,000 people took their seats. I was excited to see what all the hype was about.

Minutes later, the lights dimmed and out walked the famous technologist. His build was slight, and the stage loomed all around him like a hungry mouth as he took a bow and walked to the podium. If it hadn't been for the two screens on which his image appeared larger-than-life, I might have missed him completely. Of course, the screens also revealed his unkempt hair and rumpled tee shirt, but as I looked around to see if anyone else thought that was a problem, I observed many other people dressed similarly in this geeky crowd.

The presenter clicked a remote in his hand and began speaking, and immediately my confusion set in. The presenter's tone was flat and dull, his slides were so heavy with text and graphs that they were almost indecipherable, at least to me, and he was standing in the dark so I could barely see him at all. When he did look up, he looked directly at his slides as if we were not there. Now I really didn't get it. Was the rock concert vibe an attempt to mask just how terrible a speaker he was? Because if it was, from my perspective the attempt failed.

Though I didn't know it at the time, this presentation was a classic example of "death by PowerPoint" resulting from people spending far too much time preparing content and not nearly enough time practicing the presentation. As a performer, I couldn't understand how that could happen. After about ten minutes, my curiosity and confusion got the better of me. I elbowed the person next to me and asked, "Is this what they always do?" Imagine my surprise when he shushed me, and whispered, "He's amazing!" and returned his attention to the stage busily taking notes and hanging on every word the presenter said. Stunned at my neighbor's response, I sat back and kept my mouth shut for the remainder of the boring 45-minute keynote. At the end of the talk, when everyone got up to leave, I heard "that was fascinating!" and "I'm so glad I got a seat here this morning!" Not one person echoed my feelings.

Later that day, after talking to others about the morning's featured speaker, I remembered the Intention to *inform* is quite different from the Intention to *entertain*. The speaker knew his audience and what they wanted to hear so he gave them that Story. My confusion was a result of my own expectation of impending entertainment when I saw the big stage and lights.

In some situations, being vulnerable and knowing the audience are linked. Listeners want to know what gives the speaker joy and what they are most grateful for, what makes them cry and that they have a sense of humor, however strange.

I vividly remember the time I had the chance to witness the legendary Ella Fitzgerald perform many years ago. It was at the now-defunct Pablo Jazz Festival. Although there were many outstanding artists performing that night, I was there for her, the legend. Over the years, her music meant more to me than just a collection of recordings – it was a profound lesson on the incredible capabilities of the human voice. I was particularly fond of her rendition of "Take Love Easy" with Joe Pass. Her velvety voice, the seamless interplay between her and the guitar, and the timeless quality of her voice, which remained vibrant and youthful until the end, completely captivated me.

That night at the festival when she stepped onto the stage with her characteristic grace and prepared to sing, I was taken aback when the first words out of her mouth were, "I'm a little nervous tonight." It was unexpected, but those words had a beautiful effect – they made the audience feel closer to her, encouraged them to see her as a person rather than just a famous singer, and in a small way fostered a sense of connection.

THE BRAIN ON STORY

Since the early 2000s, businesspeople have slowly adopted the idea that sharing everyday experiences, primarily through stories, is a terrific way to get to know someone and a wonderful way to engage with an audience. But what is so special about stories? Fascinating research done by Uri Hasson and others in 2010 at Princeton University discovered that storytelling lights up the same part of the brain as story listening. This correlation falls away if the listener does not understand the story, which may explain the blank stares from the audience during many technical, academic, and science-oriented talks. This discovery underscores the impact of storytelling on audience understanding. Unless the audience comprises people from the same knowledge community, the message doesn't light us up. In his TED Talk from 2016, Hasson says, "In order for our brains to be coupled, we need common ground."

So, stories can relay common experience, but I've noted that Story is more than a timeline of events. It is an experience that captivates us. Paul Zak and his colleagues at Claremont Graduate University have identified a combination of signals in the brain they have called Immersion that measures the social-emotional value of experiences, including stories. Their studies confirm that our brains love narratives especially when they are not ordinary. They say: "Immersion is a neurologic state provoked by an experience that is unexpected, emotionally charged, narrows one's focus to the experience itself, makes the experience easy to remember, and provokes action."[23] Do we dare hope our ideas and words will have that effect on our listeners?

STORIES AS STORY

One of my favorite podcasts is the *Moth Radio Hour*. The show, which debuted in 2009, is dedicated to people sharing their stories. While some are celebrities, the vast majority are everyday people from all walks of life. It doesn't take listening to many of their shows to be inspired to consider your own experiences as story-worthy. In fact, at the end of every show, they sign off by wishing their listeners "a story-worthy week."

I've heard many people say they don't have a story to tell, but the *Moth Radio Hour* demonstrates that our lives are filled with stories. And stories are beyond culture. People around the globe from all walks of life are tuned into story patterns and rhetoric that we can all recognize. In fact, stories are part of how we experience our humanness. As the great story collector and teller Clarissa Pinkola Estes says in *Women Who Run with the Wolves*, "Stories are medicine...They have power: they do not require that we do, be, act anything – we need only listen...Stories are embedded with instructions which guide us about the complexities of life."[24]

As stated earlier, intrigue, challenges, and emotion are

---

23   Zak, Paul J. (2025 November 08). "How Stories Change the Brain." *Greater Good Magazine.* https://greatergood.berkeley.edu/article/item/how_stories_change_brain
24   Estes, Clarissa Pinkola. *Women Who Run with the Wolves.* Ballentine Books, 1996.

elements we can all choose to bring to our communication. These elements are easiest to bring to the table in the form of a story where there is an obstacle or a hurdle that has to be overcome and human interaction to which an audience can relate. As a bonus, because of the way our brains are put together, learning through stories can also enhance memory retention.[25]

A study conducted at Stanford in 1969 looked at whether chaining concepts together as in a story would improve the ability to remember them. Dr. Gordon Bower and a colleague, Michael Clark, had one group of students take lists of 10 nouns and construct stories around them, while a control group just tried to memorize the 10 words. The story constructors were later able to recall seven times as many of the words as the mere memorizers were. So, if you want to be memorable, tell a story.

Creating stories out of what needs to be memorized is an age-old technique for remembering and reciting long oral histories. Extreme memorizers also create stories out of their lists so they can remember them. Those stories are often bizarre and may make little sense to someone else, but they form a vivid image that ties words together and does what stories always do, make sense out of information.[26]

25   Hansen, Kat. (2025 November 08). "More Scientific Evidence of Story's Effectiveness: Story Learning May Enhance Memory Retention Up to Seven-fold." *A Storied Career.* http://astoriedcareer.com/more_scientific_evidence_of_st

26   Foer, Joshua. (2025 November 08). "Secrets of a Mind-gamer." *The New York Times,* February 15, 2011. https://archive.nytimes.com/www.nytimes.com/interactive/2011/02/20/magazine/mind-secrets.html

In coaching engineers and scientists, I have learned they have a lot to share about their work but often what they share is so technical and specialized that others outside of their areas of expertise cannot understand them. This is a challenge for tech companies and scientific communities who need a larger audience for their work. I've scratched my head many times trying to follow what they were talking about. However, when I've delved into their knowledge there was never a time when I couldn't find a story. It could be the story of their personal experience in their work, or about the benefits of their discoveries for others, or even a future story that imagines possibilities. If you look hard enough, there is always a story.

With the demand for more transparency in science, research stories have grown in use and popularity over the last 30 years. They now replace many research reports. What's the difference? A research *report* focuses on the method and results. A research *story* focuses on telling the narrative of the process, the significance of the research to others, and the researcher's personal experience with the research. The research story makes science more understandable and relatable to more people because although we may not understand everything a scientist does, we can all relate to being curious, facing hurdles or being surprised at a wonderful discovery.

Stories are also important in science because they are a sense-making device – call it a structure or shape – that we impose on experiences. As Hamlet tells Rosencrantz, "there is nothing either good or bad, but thinking makes it so." Experiences, events, facts, emotions, perceptions, data are neither good nor bad until we assign value to them. That value is often positioned and relayed in a narrative. In fact, an entire presentation or talk can be relayed in a narrative format. Conversely, in as little as six words we can make sense out of a situation and imply a larger story. A famous example of the latter first appeared in the early 1900s and is famously misattributed to Ernest Hemingway; "For sale: baby shoes, never worn." Another example is the shortest horror story, written by Frediric Brown in 1948. "The last man on Earth sat alone in a room. There was a knock on the door ..."

To prove their perspective on the value of narrative, in 2009, two insightful journalists, Rob Walker and Joshua Glenn, embarked on a fascinating experiment. They scoured thrift stores and garage sales, purchasing 100 random items – everything from small ornaments to old toys – often paying just a dollar or two for items dismissed as worthless.

They then engaged a group of talented storytellers to craft short narratives about each object. They paired the items with compelling stories and listed them on eBay. The result showcased the extraordinary impact of storytelling. Their original modest investment totaled around $130, but when framed with context, these items fetched nearly $8,000 in total. The power of narrative truly changed everything. And don't worry. The proceeds were donated to charity.[27]

STORY IS NOT ALWAYS STORIES

Unless we are an Einstein or a Jane Goodall, people whose work alone is worth hearing about, we may make the mistake of believing our brilliance will be enough to hold the audience for even a few minutes. Today people are used to being "revved up" by social media videos, emotionally charged movies and series, and weather reporters who are more and more like their talk-show counterparts. Fair or unfair, we all compete with entertainers for an audience's attention. To compete in this environment, we have to be prepared. Story can help.

Narrative is Story, but so is content that surprises us, evokes an emotional response and excites our grey matter.[28] Quite often this kind of Story is caused by the choice of expressions the speaker uses. I have been struck with how playful and smart many colloquial expressions can be. When you pepper these into a full narrative, Story becomes seasoned with notable flavors and accents like a spicy dish you're not likely to forget. These memorable quirks can help fuse the pathway of connection between speaker and audience.

In college, during the semester I spent in Appalachia, I was utterly charmed when I traveled to South Carolina

---

27   Gibson, William. (2025 November 08). "'Hawk' Ashtray." *Significant Objects*. https://significantobjects.com/2009/10/02/hawk-ashtray/
28   Anwart, Yasmin. (2025 November 08). "The Human Voice Can Communicate 24 Emotions." *Greater Good Magazine*. https://greatergood.berkeley.edu/article/item/the_human_voice_can_communicate_24_emotions

with some of my fellow students and stayed at the home of a friend of our professor. She welcomed us and showed us our rooms, and I could not help but notice that her phrases and choice of words were almost poetic. Apparently, this is a characteristic of South Carolinian speech. The Discover South Carolina website explains: "They play with words and invent new ones as the needs arise. They are funny without meaning to be, soulful without being maudlin, all while just getting you checked in to your hotel or serving you lunch."[29]

There was one phrase the lovely woman used that I will never forget. As she showed me to a room previously occupied by her daughter, she told me that her daughter had trouble finding a boyfriend. I don't know why she confided in me, but I loved the optimistic phrase she used to say that she was confident her daughter would find someone one day. She said, "There's not a pot so crooked that a lid won't fit." This phrase, practically a tiny story of its own, filled with hope and humor, continues to make me smile.

As in South Carolina, Story can be found in colorful phrases. It also shows up when we use metaphors. In 2012, a team of researchers from Emory University reported in Brain & Language they discovered that "when subjects in their laboratory heard a metaphor involving texture, the sensory cortex, responsible for perceiving texture through touch,

---

29   Egan, Kerry. (2025 November 08). "How to Speak South Carolinian." *Discover South Carolina.* https://discoversouthcarolina.com/articles/how-to-speak-south-carolinian#:~:-text=You'll%20notice%20pretty%20quickly,hotel%20or%20serving%20you%20lunch

became active," the sensory cortex lit up.[30] "Metaphors like 'The singer had a velvet voice' and 'He had leathery hands' roused the sensory cortex, while phrases matched for meaning, like 'The singer had a pleasing voice' and 'He had strong hands,' did not." When the sensory cortex lights up in listeners, it is noticeable.

To put this finding to good use, when preparing a presentation, we can examine our material to discover places to replace business speak with captivating expressions and colorful words. We can describe how the customer will experience the product or service. Moreover, how will it feel in their hands? Are there metaphors to use that are evocative of sensory experiences?[31]

Content that evokes an emotional response is Story, even if it's not a narrative. We all know the experience of feeling the room go quiet after someone has made a surprising remark. That quiet is an emotional response, and it is tangible. It gets our attention. It's the reaction celebrities look for when they shout out "Hello, Tokyo!" to their Tokyo audience, followed by "I can't hear you!" as they rev up the energy in the hall. It's the silent moment when the talk that struck a nerve is finished, and one could hear a pin drop just before the applause.

---

30   Emory University. (2025 November 08). "Hearing Metaphors Activates Sensory Brain Regions." *Emory News Center.* https://news.emory.edu/stories/2012/02/metaphor_brain_imaging/

31   Peters, Kate. (2011 June 17). "9 Ways to Make Your Topic Sound Exciting...Even When It's Not!" Vocal Impact. https://www.vocalimpact.net/2011/06/17/9-ways-to-make-your-topic-sound-excitingeven-when-its-not/

For a rock star, it is hard work to keep that emotional fervor going all night long but that's what is required. So, they mix it up. They may talk to the audience, bring in a surprise guest, and vary the pace of the evening's song list. For a speaker, it's usually not quite the same challenge as keeping an arena of tens of thousands engaged, but the job requires mixing those emotional moments with inflection and other elements to keep the audience paying attention to the end of the talk.

Think about theater. The curtain is about to go up. The theater goes dark, and the rumble of conversation gradually dies down as people adjust their positions in anticipation. Programs rustle, and there are a few whispers and maybe a cough. Then silence. During those moments just before the play starts, our brains light up with anticipation, we are immersed just as if we were offered a delicious piece of chocolate or about to receive a reward. We are excited, but mostly we are curious. We can't wait to know what comes next.

What if people felt this same excitement when you gave a talk or a presentation? That delightful response can be activated within the first few minutes of a speech with something called an empowerment promise. An empowerment promise hints about what's coming, promising the listener they will learn something new, even something surprising or unexpected.

Years ago, speakers used jokes called ice breakers to grab their audience's attention. Usually, the joke had nothing to do with the talk or the speaker. Jokes can be fun, but connection occurs when the audience can relate to the anecdote being told, so a favorite joke is not as effective as something that happened on the way to work. Better yet, we should ask, "What is fascinating or titillating to this audience?" and create Story around that.

Curiosity is fundamental to humans. Although different people are curious about different things and to different degrees, scientists have shown that our curiosity about learning something new is akin to the pleasurable curiosity we feel when the curtain is about to go up. This kind of wonder is called "epistemic curiosity." It is associated with good feelings and positive neural responses, which is why it is such a great addition to the opening of a presentation. The promise of empowering an audience with something not previously known is Story because it ignites the desire within them to learn and keeps them wanting to hear more.

Another way to create Story is helping our audience to feel involved with our ideas. For businesspeople, a call to action that connects directly to the presentation and drives home what we want the audience to do with what they've learned can be Story. A good call to action therefore is Story in action. It galvanizes the Intention and captures the hearts and minds of listeners. It answers the question, "What do I want the audience to do now?" Every good presentation or conversation deserves a good call to action, and every audience wants one. Time is precious and we are all competing for it.

I learned the importance of a strong call to action when I logged into a Zoom meeting to provide feedback to a dry run of an important presentation a client was going to give. Her entire team was on the call to help fine tune the final product. The talk was a keynote to be delivered to a large group and it highlighted several meaningful advances in human rights that had been accomplished by the organization represented by my client and the audience which was made up of vendors. The message was clear – together we've done a lot to improve people's lives. It was good news and much of which they could be proud. The rehearsal progressed well enough. My client knew her business and she delivered the content without a hitch.

But something was off. I had the feeling that the whole team was avoiding what they really wanted to say. Even though they all helped to build the presentation, it was somehow wrong. There was palpable dissatisfaction with the final slides, and the message wandered as it got toward the end. There was an uneasy undertow, as if something was drawing the team away from the message they really wanted to convey.

I have learned that a story needs to include an obstacle which the protagonist has to overcome. I have seen many businesses fail to capture their audience with their pitch because they were afraid to talk about mistakes or difficulties undergone. So, I asked, "What are the hurdles you face together to accomplish more?"

That's when we realized the team was avoiding the one thing they really wanted to say: "If you don't do more to help women get better jobs and advance in their careers, we will no longer do business together."

That was a pretty tough message but getting clear about their Intention allowed them to go back and clarify and rewrite some of the content which led to a firm conclusion reflecting a call to action about gender equity.

When it comes to effective closings, I was once told that Barbra Streisand only sang one high note per show so that people would always leave wanting more. I've never found written evidence of this, but let's say it's true. That's a story about Story. Often, we want to pack everything we can imagine about a topic into a presentation or talk when it may be best to be more selective. This goes for the closing as well. In speaking as in singing, less is more. Even better if the less is captivating. Since we can't all sing a single high note that leaves people wanting more we can still give them what they want.

Stories should always be reinforced with an effective closing. While Story can reside in an empowerment promise at the beginning, piqued throughout the presentation via emotional cues, colorful phrasing, or curiosity, and rallied through a call to action, the audience should have a sense of closure at the end. An effective closing may summarize key points you made. It could be a reminder of your call to action. It could be a recap of why your solution/product/strategy is right for the problem at hand. The point is an effective closing 'closes' the loop of your story; it ends the narrative with satisfying resolve.

THE INTENTIONAL STORY

Story begins with Intention. Each component of this triad — Intention, Story, Presence — influences the others in a virtuous cycle that I call Reverberation ... but if I had to pick a point of origin, it would be Intention. Thinking back to our section on Intention, our Intention may vary according to circumstances. In telling Story we might want to teach a lesson, gain support for a course of action, or we just might want to entertain.

A dear friend of mine was involved in a terrible automobile accident and was surprised to find that she did not end up in heaven. While driving through an intersection, another driver T-boned her car, causing the driver's side to cave in. My friend was thrown forcibly to the passenger side of the front seat. In that moment, her first thought was, *Did I tell my mom that I love her?*

Initially, as she shared her incident, her Intention was to relay what had happened and express her disbelief at having escaped death. A few days later, she recounted a cautionary tale about the severity of the accident and her frustration with dealing with insurance companies. A couple of weeks later, her purpose in retelling the event shifted to recommending an excellent physical therapist to her colleague. Although all versions shared the same core events, the details changed to reflect her different Intentions.

As we discussed in the last chapter, Intention is many-layered. A larger, personal Intention will inform Story, too. That's what happened with Les. I met Les in April 2016 when he participated in a workshop that I developed for his company. He was one of their top lawyers, but he showed up as reserved, even shy. He described himself as a little too self-conscious, but wanting to have more impact as a leader. Overall, he was a nice guy, warm, and open to what I had to say and what we did in the workshop.

A month later, he hired me as his coach. When we started working together, he created a statement of Intention, an aim to guide our work together. I don't usually share the statements because they are personal, but Les gave me permission to share his. Here it is:

> *My Intention is to be a caring, fair, impactful leader who is focused on making a positive difference at work, in my community, and in the world. I educate, inspire, and motivate others to bring to reality my vision of unlocking the passion we all have for doing great things.*

Our work together was to manifest that Intention — to bring it into reality so that he would inspire and motivate others and, in turn, begin to show their passion for doing great things at work and also in their personal lives. This was a tall order for someone who was reserved and self-conscious, but it was clearly why he hired me.

That year, his organization aggressively aimed to increase career satisfaction to 80%. He wanted to see it happen because he deeply believed that though this would be good for the organization, it would be even better for its people. He knew he had an opportunity and a responsibility to help management figure out how to do this, and it would require more from him in talks and conversations. In addition, he wasn't all that comfortable with public speaking.

He quickly became a student of why people enjoy their work, what motivates them, and what leaders can do to create an environment where people thrive. This is when I discovered his superpower: He was passionate about learning, a true autodidact. He came up with facts and figures, graphs and charts and many reasons why people thrive or don't thrive at work. He quoted statistics and generously shared his ideas with his colleagues.

Because of his enthusiasm, an opportunity came up to give a talk to managers. He created a presentation with some extremely convincing points based on his research, but it was dry so, I suggested he add a story. He said, "I'm not sure anyone would be interested in my stories." I pressed him further and after much consideration, he finally decided he could add a story about a mentor who had been important to him. It was a good story, and he planned to use it to illustrate his learning about motivation.

Sometimes we accept a good story as good enough. Most stories are enough to connect because stories are conduits in and of themselves. In Les's case, as often happens, telling the story of his mentor reminded him of another story; he told me about his mom and how she started the first recycling center in the Pacific Northwest. He talked about how she was also a lifelong learner and a writer who had been so passionate about her work that she fulfilled her dream of publishing not one but two books while fighting colon cancer at the end of her life.

After a quiet moment, I said, "Tell that story."

Surprised, he asked, "Really? The story about my mom? But this is a business presentation."

I replied, "Just this once. Try it."

With some hesitation, as this story was even more personal than the one about his mentor, he agreed. After his talk, he got an email from a colleague who wrote: "Your talk was really outstanding. I loved the story about your mom, and I can't think of another presentation I've ever heard on management from which I learned more or enjoyed more. Thanks for taking the time to put it together and to share it. I think if you were everyone's manager, our goal would be easily surpassed."

LISTENING TO CONNECT

Although Intentional stories do a good job of illustrating purpose, we cannot fully engage another human being without knowing something about who they are and what they care about. As we saw with Les, we need common interests and vivid mental imagery that illuminate and support our Intention. But, if Story is going to connect, we must be willing to listen before we speak.

Our choice of words in everyday speech indicates preferences for how we learn and what we believe. Choices in language are transparent indicators of how we see the world. Thus, listening closely to stories that others relate and the words they use to describe their experiences gives us hints about what matters to them and what they want to hear from us.

Another part of listening involves listening to ourselves. What words do we use to describe our world? Often, we use words connected to our preferred sensory modality. The acronym VARK stands for the four sensory modalities — Visual, Aural, Read/write, and Kinesthetic — and we all have a preferred sensory system. For example, my preferred sense is aural. I remember directions, names, and numbers best if I say them aloud. A preferred modality may also show up when we write. I find that I often say, "I want you to hear this" when the person will actually read or see it.

In addition to sensory preferences, words illustrate our biases, how we experience relationships and see the world around us. Years ago, I was facilitating a workshop for a group of HR executives. I told a story about someone gaining prowess as a leader who appeared stronger and taller after we worked together. One of the HR leaders raised her hand and posed a thought-provoking idea. "You are biased about leadership," she said. "You think people must be tall and strong to be good leaders. What about a soft-spoken woman in a wheelchair? What kind of leader do you think she would be?"

The HR person's observation caught me off guard. I was not aware of this bias, but she was right. I thanked her for her challenge, and it was a transformative moment for me. I absolutely believed a woman like that could be a good leader, so it was time to change my description of leadership. I resolved to study my language and root out the hidden biases as much as possible or own them. This recognition of biases through the words we use is a powerful tool that we can all use to expose hidden beliefs or feelings. Taking stock of how we describe the world can ensure that we show up how we want to.

It is possible to listen to ourselves to hear how others hear us and better understand what's going on within our own minds. What stories do we tell over and over? What are our favorite phrases? How do we respond to others when they speak to us? Do we say we invite conversation, but find ourselves holding court in a group? Are we curious about others? What words do we use to describe our lives? Story with a capital S is conscious and chosen to reflect both our Intention and Presence. Listening to ourselves and others gives us the awareness that allows us to increase our impact on the world.

Although many behaviors can improve listening, one of the best is simply asking more questions and giving less advice. This is especially important for leaders. But doesn't being a leader mean speaking to people, giving guidance, and telling others what they need to do to meet goals? Perhaps so, but good listening instills trust and loyalty in others because the act alone demonstrates empathy. According to Dr. Rick Fulwiler, Harvard T.H. Chan School of Public Health, "Listening is one of the most important communication skills there is, yet most of us have had little or no formal training in listening... Listening is highly active, requiring us to use not only our ears but our head, heart, eyes and body."[32]

We can make listening more effective, increase collaboration, experience more engaged communication partners, and enjoy better retention of what we hear by focusing on the Intention to listen and hear. We may need to use tools and develop other skills to increase our ability to actually hear what others say. For example, taking notes while listening can help us focus as will forcing ourselves to listen well enough to repeat what we've heard. Starting with a clear Intention to listen will greatly improve our ability to connect with our audiences and to have productive and meaningful interactions.

SELLING OR BEING SOLD

DemandSage notes in their 2025 startup statistics that

---

32 Fulwiler, Richard. "Transformational Leadership: The Key to World-Class Safety." *EHS Today*. June 2011.

 **INSIGHT**

Listening LifeHack #1: Message paraphrasing and encouraging speaker elaboration communicates understanding and interest. Instead of immediately giving advice when speaking with colleagues and employees, be quiet and inquisitive, and take notes if needed. Try these questions (from *The Book of Beautiful Questions* by Warren Berger[1]):

1. What else?
2. Just to be clear, is this what you are saying? (Paraphrase what you've heard.)
3. Can you explain what you mean by that?

Listening Lifehack #2: Stop multitasking while listening. Some research suggests that multitasking can reduce productivity by as much as 40% rather than improve it.[2] Instead, give the other person your full attention to avoid a hit to your productivity and retention, and take notes. Then ask questions (See Listening Lifehack #1).

Listening Lifehack #3: Set aside your opinions and judgments and listen without preparing to jump in with your own POV. Working with people who have different perspectives or areas of expertise can result in better ideas and results. It may even increase innovation. Practice intellectual humility. Being a more collaborative listener helps create an environment where others feel respected, valued, and comfortable being themselves.[3]

---

1   https://amorebeautifulquestion.com/the-book-of-beautiful-questions/
2   Cherry, Kendra. (2025 November 08). "How Multitasking Affects Productivity and Brain Health." *VeryWellMind*. https://www.verywellmind.com/multitasking-2795003
3   Stone, Emily. (2025 November 08). "The Science Behind the Growing Importance of Collaboration." *KellogInsight*. https://insight.kellogg.northwestern.edu/article/the-science-behind-the-growing-importance-of-collaboration

there are "more than 150 million startups worldwide." They also note that "50 million new startups are established every year. That means, on average 137,000 startups are launched every day."[33] It's an exciting time, and the world is full of possibility. However, amidst this sea of new ideas, the real challenge lies in getting someone to listen, let alone buy. After all, you cannot make someone want to hear you.

Now, the problem with exciting possibilities is that we can get so caught up in selling our ideas that we fail to create a real connection. An example is the "used-car salesman" persona, the stereotype of a slick, falsely friendly, pushy salesperson. In fact, I've often felt that salespeople who sell the highest-priced items, such as technology, run the risk of being seen as insincere because their Intention to persuade others to buy high-ticket products can earn such great rewards. However, great salespeople know that setting the Intention to build relationships is more potent than the Intention to make a sale.

Social media has proven the power of relationship-building in sales. Influencers, for instance, establish a Presence and freely share advice on topics like makeup application or car repair. Their value is measured by their followers. Once they become valuable to product brands, they are paid to endorse those brands on their social media channels, always within the context of their established expertise.

---

33   Kumar, Naveen. (2025 November 08). "Startup Statistics (2025): Numbers By Country & Success Rates." Demandsage. https://www.demandsage.com/startup-statistics/

The approach has been quite successful in the universe of the Internet, where the "freemium" often builds followers. However, the impact goes away when the influencer doesn't align with the product they promote. This was the case with fashion blogger Chriselle Lim, who suddenly became eco-conscious when she was hired by Volvo to promote their eco-friendly car wash product. Her fans were suspicious of the change because even though she promoted other products, everyone knew how the game was played. This campaign was too obviously about selling. The trust placed in both her brand and Volvo's was suddenly in question, highlighting the potential pitfalls of not aligning Intention and Story.

The degree of impact or influence is determined by the degree of alignment between the Intention, the Story, and the Presence. This alignment is crucial and provides a guide to creating a Story and shaping a Presence. When someone thinks of their authority as persuasive, such as a salesman might, and they focus primarily on persuasion, they must demonstrate a terrific expertise in persuasion. However, when the Intention is to persuade others to support an idea, their authority as the creator of the concept takes the spotlight.

When we come up with an idea, and it is developed enough to present to others, we usually have a great deal we could say about it, and often too much. Engineers are notorious for getting into so many details that audiences of non-engineers lose interest. A huge benefit of knowing our audience is we can start with an Intention that clarifies ways to use Story more effectively. We can be more discerning about what is most essential for our audience to hear out of all that we could say about our ideas.

FINDING STORIES

We are all storytellers. It's part of being human. However, when asked to tell a story I've observed that many people respond with, "I don't have any good stories" or "I don't know any." That same person might go home from work and tell their spouse the story of their day. I've learned that is because most people, like my friend Les, don't think their own stories are interesting.

A colleague of mine told me that he realized the power of storytelling early in his career when he was supporting a marketing organization for a major oil company. He was an English major who found his niche in communications. The team he was supporting was working on a rebranding effort for one of their customer-facing products. He was helping the Marketing VP put together a presentation explaining their strategy. As they worked through the deck, the VP asked, "What's our storyline?" My friend was taken aback for a moment. He thought they were working on a business strategy, why was she talking about storylines? Weren't storylines the business of literature?

It then dawned on him that she was referring to the train of logic which moved them from strategic drivers to market implications to potential solutions. Their storyline was made up of the answers to key questions like: *What context were we operating in? What led us to this point? Where were we heading?* Indeed, he thought, what was their story?

As an English major, my friend knew stories. He knew what comprised them and he knew a wide variety of ways to organize them. He could do this, he realized. He could tell stories, and if he could tell stories, he could build strategies. From that moment on he has never looked back. He has since led an exciting and successful career as a corporate communicator doing what English majors love best – telling stories.

As my friend discovered, asking questions is a great way to find a story. The questions that help find a story involve inquiry around the human experience. To find stories for *The Moth* directors ask storytellers, "What are moments from your life, big or small, that stick with you?" Later in the story development process they may ask, "Was there a time when you discovered you were stronger than you thought," or "realized that you were just plain wrong?"

With some genuine curiosity we can dig deep into our lives and find stories to tell. In business, people often have themes about which they create a presentation or a meeting. Using the theme, a great question to ask is "Was there a time when I personally experienced [the theme]?" After considering some salient questions, over and over I've seen people come up with a story even though they've said they don't have any.

One of the most essential features of making a story into

Story is its ability to be meaningful to the listener. Without shared experiences or relatable themes, the listener's brain remains inactive, making it challenging for a connection to form. This scenario is especially true for engineers and scientists who often find themselves needing to communicate complex ideas to those without technical backgrounds.

Enter Kai, an engineer with a profound understanding of computer systems — so ingrained in his knowledge that he often compared it to knowing the back of his hand. His work was intricate, involving subtle adjustments that could

---

 **EXERCISE**

How to Find a Personal Story for a Business Presentation

1. Pick a topic such as growth, change, discovery, etc. Was there another time in your life when you experienced that topic? What happened? Tell that story.
2. What moments of your life stick with you? What happened then? Tell that story.
3. Let your mind drift for a moment as you think about your topic. What comes up for you? When did you feel that way before? Tell that story.
4. Be transparent about your struggles. Look deep into moments of your life that were filled with self-doubt, uncertainty, too many choices or not enough choices. What did you do? How did you feel? Tell that story.
5. Discover your a-ha moments. Think back to a time when you learned or realized something important. Tell that story.

unravel monumental technology challenges, particularly in the realms of security and artificial intelligence. Along with his technical prowess, Kai possessed an outgoing and warm personality, making him exceptionally skilled at fostering collaboration and exchanging innovative ideas. Yet, when we first met, he faced a new daunting challenge. He had recently been promoted to a role requiring him to present and communicate his concepts to an executive team, a group well-versed in business but lacking in technical insight. Their busy schedules left little room for deep dives into the complexities of his work, making it critical for Kai to adapt his communication style.

Years of hard work had earned him respect within his field, complemented by a plethora of patents. However, this did not shield him from the need for greater support for his initiatives. To accomplish this, Kai had to convey his technical narrative in an accessible manner, enabling non-technical audiences to grasp the significance of his work.

We began our journey by focusing on Intention and swiftly transitioned into the art of storytelling. Together, we reviewed the presentations he had crafted, dissecting key concepts and terminology. I prompted him to recall any stories that resonated with these concepts — anything from personal experiences to anecdotal tales. To my delight, Kai had a wealth of captivating stories to draw from — an array of experiences that ranged from his professional achievements to poignant reflections on his family and his journey from

South America. However, as we delved deeper, I sensed his hesitancy. Like many engineers, when describing his ideas he felt most at ease articulating meticulous details rather than narrating a more generalized version that he believed might seem diluted or inaccurate. I took a moment to explain the reality: His technical jargon was foreign to his audience, akin to speaking a different language altogether. Without a shift in how he shared his insights, he risked losing their engagement and support entirely. I firmly believed that harnessing the power of storytelling could bridge this gap.

Then, during one enlightening session, Kai excitedly announced he had been invited to speak at an international conference filled with engineers — peers who shared his technical background. We dedicated our time to refining his talk, preparing him for the audience awaiting him across the ocean, and I eased up on my insistence that he find stories about his ideas. After all he would be speaking to a group who spoke his engineering language.

A week later, he entered our session beaming with enthusiasm. "How was your talk?" I asked, eager to hear his experience. With a sparkle in his eyes, he replied, "I practiced it over and over until it felt just right. But on the day of the conference, I made a bold decision — I opted to set my formal talk aside. I thought, *What better time than now to test the potential of storytelling?* So, I took the leap. When it was my turn, instead of adhering strictly to my notes, I stepped away from the lectern, requested that my slides not be shown, pulled a chair close to the edge of the stage, and sat down. Then, I shared a story."

As he recounted this moment, I could almost envision the scene – the bright lights of the auditorium, the expectant audience leaning forward in their seats, intrigued. He continued, "I noticed a ripple of laughter as I shared my first story, and that gave me the encouragement to continue. I weaved in narratives about technology and my new ideas, infusing them with personal anecdotes, and Kate, it was incredible. They listened intently, they engaged with me, and they understood what I was conveying. But more importantly, it unlocked bringing my whole self to my stories including my accent and smiles."

Kai's transformation was evident, and it underscored the powerful impact of storytelling – it bridged the gap between the technical and the relatable, allowing him to connect deeply, even with an audience of peers. He now could see what it would do for an audience of executives.

The questions that reveal stories are often those that make us think about a situation from a different perspective. For example, a technologist might ask herself, "Can you imagine the possibilities of what this will do for other people? What will their experience be when they use it?" The latter question would be particularly important for those whose solutions are embedded deep within the systems we use. Most of us will never know they are there in our phones or navigation systems, but they will make a difference in our experience, and that is what we care about.

Scientists are also finding the power in Story.[34] Using a story arc, they can create a narrative about the human experience in research, whether the experience of the researcher or the participant in the research. The use of stories in science is, however, something whose value is debated by scientists. Although it's generally agreed that stories help non-scientists better understand science, just like engineers, many scientists feel stories too often reflect a distorted view of reality and facts and contribute to misinformation. However, science has been on the chopping block in recent years and the rise in the focus on telling science stories is a direct response to that threat. If science is to get the funding it needs, it must be understood by non-scientists who are largely the funders. Connection with the audience is of critical importance.

PUTTING IT ALL TOGETHER

At the beginning of this chapter, we discussed what Story with a capital S is. To review, it is stories with a narrative arc, of course, but it can also include phatic communication that reveals small but important details about the speaker. Story is also the use of techniques such as emotional appeals, expressive words, and calls to action. All of these and many others can lead to engagement with others. Using

---

34 Miami University. (2025 November 08). "Research Stories." Howe Writing Center. https://www.miamioh.edu/hcwe/handouts/research-stories/index.html

this information, we can let our voices be heard in talks, presentations, and conversations that keep others interested while providing factual information even if the audience doesn't speak our jargon.

To use Story, we may need to create new models for communication. Here's one model for such a talk. Notice how the sections with data are sandwiched between Story:

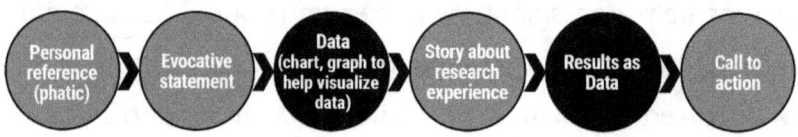

The most important part of the model above is that Story in the form of stories and choice of words is inserted between chunks of information to keep people engaged enough to hear the data. In addition, increased vocal inflection, a vocal element of Presence which will be covered in the next chapter, can be added to increase engagement. We may not even have to work very hard at the latter.

It is a natural tendency for people to become noticeably more expressive with their voice and body language when telling a story. This is partially due to the chemicals released in the body when we engage in storytelling. When it comes to vocal changes, the magic ingredients are Dopamine and oxytocin. Dopamine modulation is linked to vocalization. [35]

35   Turk, Ariana Z., Mahsa Lotfi Marchoubeh, Ingrid Fritsch, Gerald A. Maguire, Shahriar SheikhBahaei. "Dopamine, Vocalization, and Astrocytes." *Brain and Language*. Volume 219, 2021, 104970, ISSN 0093-934X. https://doi.org/10.1016/j.bandl.2021.104970 (https://www.sciencedirect.com/science/article/pii/S0093934X2100064X)

For example, low amounts of Dopamine are thought to lead to the characteristic speech changes of Parkinson's, such as monotone and soft speech, and very high levels of Dopamine are related to stuttering. Oxytocin is also responsible for several neural processes underlying speech production, including controlling the use of pitch, rhythm, and intensity to convey emotions in speech.

HOW TO REMEMBER THE STORY

I have a friend who loves to tell stories but always forgets the important parts, like the reason he was telling the story in the first place, or the punch line. Another friend has stories he wants to share but has trouble remembering anything but the main theme. As a musician, I am quite comfortable with memorization. I've observed that when I am singing something I've spent time preparing, I can see the page of music in my mind's eye.

My technique is simple: I study the music and practice it, and, fortunately, fairly quickly begin to realize that it is holding in my memory. In traditional music, there is often a story that goes with the music, told through the words or the notes and that makes memorization easier. But I often perform pieces that are non-traditional, even avant-garde. Because of that, I learned to create my own approach to memorization for these more complex works.

In the 1990s, I had the privilege of working with composer Edward Barnes who composed songs and several short dramatic pieces for me. One of them, "Old Aunt Dinah's Sure Guide to Dreams and Lucky Numbers," was based on a book of numbers that Edward found in an antique store in New Orleans. My character was a wise-woman, earth spirit, and sorceress (most likely a con artist) who doled out advice on the gaining of riches and love, the significance of dreams and the divination of the future. The score called for memorization of long lists of words and numbers. At first it was a bit daunting to remember the exact order of words such as those in this list from a scene called "Love Charm."[36]

> *The heart's the key,*
> *The core*
> *The grain*
> *The grit*
> *The seed*
> *The spore*
> *The blood*
> *The beat*
> *The pulse*
> *The force*
> *The temper*
> *The center*
> *The fire*
> *The nucleus of love.*

Edward used assonance in his lyrics and that helped, and

---

36 Barnes, Edward. "Love Charm." *Old Aunt Dinah's Sure Guide To Dreams & Lucky Numbers.* https://www.edwbarnes.com/ed-barnes-website/composer

normally remembering a melody or harmonic structure to which the words attach is helpful. However, there was little variation in the accompanying music, so I couldn't remember simply through a change in notes. He didn't make it easy for me. Since I have a passion for singing new music and it is often non-traditional in its harmonic and melodic structure, I've had to rely on three things to help me memorize music. The first is pattern recognition. The second is physical movement, and the third is speaking or singing aloud as I learn rather than merely going over it in my head.

The wonderful choreography by Kimi Okada, School Director and Associate Choreographer for ODC made a difference because although I learned the piece before rehearsal, the moves brought it all together. With each step or gesture, I could attach a word, while the movement secured the word and notes in my memory. Movement can also help speakers remember content. Studies of superior memorizers using fMRI's while they are memorizing numbers show increased activity in the spatial areas of the brain.[37] This could explain why it's easier to remember a talk that has been "blocked" as when stage movements are added to a dramatic piece. Although speakers may not wish to be choreographed, assigning a step or a turn of the head to words or topics while preparing for a talk can bring those items to mind enough to

---

37   Mallow, J., Bernarding, J., Luchtmann, M., Bethmann, A., Brechmann, A. "Superior Memorizers Employ Different Neural Networks for Encoding and Recall." *Front Syst Neurosci.* 2015 Sep 14;9:128. doi: 10.3389/fnsys.2015.00128. PMID: 26441560; PMCID: PMC4568341.

make a script or a teleprompter unnecessary.

I don't generally recommend people write and memorize speeches. Today, people want a more casual approach to presenting rather than formal, meticulously crafted speeches. However, we still need to memorize structure, some details of our points and stories, and some people just feel more confident when they have memorized sections of their presentations and talks. So, let's discuss a time-tested method for memorization.

Not everyone finds memorization easy. For this reason, I was fascinated and encouraged when I came upon the "memory palace." If this concept sounds familiar it may because it has been popularized by several larger-than-life characters such as Sherlock Holmes as well as maybe his polar opposite Hannibal Lector. This is a mnemonic technique used by orators in ancient Greece. It was rediscovered by Mateo Ricci in the late 17th century. Ricci used the technique to make Catholicism memorable to the Chinese. While we could argue that it didn't work out so well for Ricci, still it's a great tool and one that I find very helpful. The basic approach is to create a mental picture of a familiar setting, and "place" reminders of what we are trying to remember throughout the mental picture. To recall what we need to remember, we simply "walk" through the setting, and it is all there.

The Memory Palace is used by memory athletes, those people who can memorize thousands of random digits in under an hour. Most of them say that anyone can do what they

 **EXERCISE**

Making your own Memory Palace

First, make your "palace." Imagine the interior of a building such as your home or office. It doesn't have to be palatial. Pick a particular room, one that has lots of places to tuck things in corners or on tables and shelves. I use the foyer of a former residence because it is spacious with lots of nooks, areas to put things, and entrances to rooms. But your building could be anything you choose. It could even be a garden or a favorite haunt.

Once you've created your palace, create a list of ten items you want to remember. You might start with a grocery list. Here's one you can use:

1. Eggs
2. Bacon
3. Matches
4. Lettuce
5. Shoelaces
6. Butter
7. Soap
8. Almonds
9. Chocolate
10. Flour

Next, set a timer for two minutes, scan the list and create a vivid image for each item. The images should be ridiculous, absurd, bright, and bold – anything but boring. In your mind's eye, place one image by the door as you enter your room. Gradually place all the images in different places as you walk throughout the room. When the time is up, put away the list and test yourself to see what you remember.

do, but that it takes learning to "think in new ways." It starts with excellent focus that is followed by lavish mental images that are difficult to forget. The images may be ludicrous, or vulgar, or exciting, validation of the Immersion work of Paul Zak and his colleagues.

Memorization involves practice and when it comes to practicing talks and presentations, many people express a concern about over-rehearsing. They worry that too much practice may make them sound overly polished or studied. This raises the question: Can you rehearse too much or too little? Is there a specific amount of time that guarantees peak readiness? In music, we have scales, exercises, and pieces to practice that help us develop our skills and agility as performers. Similarly, in public speaking and presenting, we can engage in exercises designed to enhance our awareness and the skills we need. Some of these exercises focus on physical and mental aspects, much like music practice, while others adapt similar techniques towards different goals.

As a musician, I recognize the importance of practice to improve my skills. I learned how to practice when I was seven years old. With my violin, music stand, sheet music, and a timer, I would shut the door to my room and dedicate an hour each day to playing my exercises and pieces. During my lessons, I focused on various aspects of my instrument to enhance my ability to discern tone, pitch, and intonation.

Today, after years of study and performance, I have trained my ears to appreciate the different elements that make up a voice, including individual characteristics and subtle changes influenced by Intention, as well as issues that indicate vocal problems. Much of my rehearsal occurs in a private space, with the door closed or far from others. However, for business professionals, practicing public speaking in private can often be challenging. As a result, many of them find themselves pacing around their offices, thinking about what they want to say instead of practicing aloud.

Tom was an architect who had relocated to Scotland with his family for a year, immersing himself in a significant architectural project. The four of them were cozily settled into a modest two-bedroom flat. While deep in the design realm, Tom had seldom engaged in articulating his thoughts about his work, preferring to let his designs speak for themselves. Now, however, he found himself facing the daunting task of speaking in front of large audiences — a challenge that left him feeling anxious. A key obstacle was his self-consciousness about rehearsing his presentations in front of others. His office lacked the seclusion he craved, leading him to wander the hallways, contemplating his speeches silently rather than practicing them aloud. This approach, however, didn't serve him well during his presentations, where his intended messages often got lost in translation.

After enduring several underwhelming presentations, Tom mustered the courage to seek guidance on how and when to practice effectively. In response I encouraged him to dedicate at least 10 to 15 minutes daily to practice exercises that involved an amusing array of sounds — everything from silly lip bubbles to nonsensical phrases and even exaggerated heavy breathing as well as the content for his talks and presentations. Faced with a lack of privacy, we reviewed his daily routine and discovered a golden opportunity: a ten-minute walk to the train station, where he typically encountered very few people. At first, even with the low chances of running into anyone, practicing aloud felt strange and exposed. Each time he spotted another person on his route, he would abruptly halt his vocalizations, waiting for them to pass, his cheeks tinged with embarrassment. However, after he experienced the unmistakable improvement in his presentations that resulted from actually vocalizing his practice, he became increasingly motivated to integrate warm-up routines and posture exercises into his daily walks. Gradually, after a month of this unconventional practice, he found himself shedding his initial reservations. The potential judgment of strangers became inconsequential; he was now fully convinced that the benefits of dedicated practice far outweighed his pride.

When it comes to practicing, I suggest using creative solutions to find the right time and place. Consider finding a secluded outdoor space or reserving a conference room. Build time into your day at work and also at home. While rehearsing in one room at home, you can increase the volume of the TV or stereo in a different room to avoid worrying about being overheard. And, for your first run-through, the best audience might be your family pet. A dry run can help you work out any issues, and pets are usually much more forgiving than humans.

REFLECTION
STORMS AND PERFECT STORMS

While compelling content can be powerful, its impact is diminished when it stands alone. In the world of seafaring, there are both storms and perfect storms. When used in alignment with Intention, Story can produce remarkable results. However, rather than being a destructive force, I believe the power of Story is that it is directed toward connection with others for constructive purposes. The best way to ensure this is to become aware of how we present ourselves and whether we are aligned with our Intention and Story. To that end, we will dig into the concept of Presence.

CHAPTER 3

THE THIRD PRINCIPLE, **PRESENCE**

"No matter how you feel, get up, dress up, and show up."

– Regina Brett

 **WHAT YOU WILL LEARN**

CHAPTER 3: PRESENCE

How you show up before you say a word.

What You'll Learn
- What Presence is — and what it's not.
- How breath, body, and voice align to create Presence.
- How vocal image is part of Presence.
- How to become aware of (and overcome) Presence blockers.
- Simple practices to become more grounded, resonant, and engaged.

Key Takeaways
- Presence is your energy in the room — it speaks before your words do.
- You can develop Presence just like any skill — with practice and awareness.
- The way you sound influences Presence just as much as what you say.
- Grounded, embodied Presence creates real-time influence.

UNDERSTANDING PRESENCE

If I were to ask the average businessperson to tell me what the core of a presentation is, they would likely say: "It's the slide deck." If I asked a performer, they would answer, "It's the person presenting." If I asked a writer, they might quote Shakespeare's *Hamlet*: "Words, words, words." That is, it's the content.

To be fair, they are all correct; however, there is always a person at the center. It is a person who speaks the words and explains the presentation. A person who brings the message to life not only through slides and words but through gestures, movement, tone, and expressions. In a sense, the person embodies the message. They might say of themselves, "I am the message."

I had a speaking engagement with a group of government employees and because of my mixed feelings about PowerPoint, I decided to deliver my talk without slides. However, as I watched others present ahead of me, I noticed the audience taking pictures of the screens. I started to doubt my decision, questioning whether the audience would understand my points without visual aids. Despite my initial hesitation, my talk went well, and the audience's attention was tangible. The workshop I offered later in the day was so popular that they had to bring in extra chairs. I concluded that I had been correct – people want to hear from other people not slides.

An executive client once told me that the second most

unexpected thing she learned from our work together was how she, as a person, made an impression on a room simply by walking into it. Regardless of what she may be thinking and regardless of whether she wanted the attention, people noticed. Not only did they notice, but they read and judged her in an instant. To her relief, she also learned that she had control over those impressions, that she could influence what people thought about her before she uttered a word.

Many people are daunted by the idea that others "read" us merely by seeing us. Admittedly, it can be disconcerting to learn that for the first 30 seconds that someone speaks, people assess who they are and decide whether to keep listening. Yet, this isn't just a feeling; it is a fact. In 1967 Dr. Albert Mehrabian showed that only 7% of what others understand when we communicate feelings is in the words we say.[38] The other 93% comes from paralanguage, or how we say what we say through our posture, gestures, and voice. The term I use to capture this idea is Presence. Presence is not just a theory, it is a practice. And as a practice there are principles and tools that can help us shape our Presence, making us more comfortable with "being the message."

The common definition of Presence is the bearing, carriage, or air that a person projects. It is often described as a noteworthy quality of poise or effectiveness. While Presence is most often discussed in the context of corporate

---

38   Mehrabian, A. Silent Messages: Implicit Communication of Emotions and Attitudes. Wadsworth, 1981.

and entertainment arenas, it is also prevalent in education, politics, and in our everyday lives.

In the business world, we refer to "Executive Presence." Generally, observers describe a leader with strong Executive Presence as displaying charisma, or that indescribable "certain something" that some people have because "they were just born that way." However, COQUAL, a research group in New York City, found it is much more tangible than that. They explain that Executive Presence is "an amalgam of qualities that true leaders exude, a Presence that telegraphs you're in charge or deserve to be." Interestingly, after surveying hundreds of executives, they further concluded that Executive Presence can be broken down into specific qualities, with the core being "gravitas" which is commonly defined as "dignity, seriousness, or solemnity of manner."[39]

In the teaching world, Presence is said to have three different variations — Social Presence, Teaching Presence, and Cognitive Presence — all of which are essential for successful instruction.[40] On a less scholarly level, most people can recall a teacher they once had who had a distinctive Presence, be it commanding or caring or, the best of all, "cool." Even in our post-Covid world of virtual classrooms, Presence continues to have a tremendous impact on students.

In politics, a candidate with well-defined Presence may

39   Coqual. "Executive Presence: Key Findings." *Coqual* (formerly CTI), 2013. https://coqual.org/reports/executive-presence/
40   Northeastern. (2025 November 08). "Teaching Presence in the Community of Inquiry Framework." Northeastern Center for Advancing Teaching and Learning Through Research. https://learning.northeastern.edu/teaching-presence/

have an edge over one without. In the U.S. general election in November of 1960, John F. Kennedy took a narrow lead over Richard Nixon and won the presidency. It is largely held that Kennedy's effortless, elegant style persuaded people to vote for him. Controversial and famously charismatic, another leader well-known for his Presence is one of the most decorated managers in European football, José Mourinho who hails from Portugal and was dubbed "The Special One" by British press. The moniker refers to his winnings as well as the way he uses his charming and persuasive communication skills to influence.

Personally, I believe Presence is available to anyone, not just executives, teachers, celebrities or politicians. Some people do indeed seem to create charismatic Presence naturally, but Presence is a choice. It reflects how we decide to show up and, as such, the first definition of Presence as "the bearing, carriage or air that a person projects" stands as the most accurate.

The kind of Presence we think of as appealing and positive is the result of a desire to bring our ideas to the table and the confidence to do so. It develops as we learn to trust that we indeed have something to say. Presence is a personification of a commitment to one's thoughts and ideas, and for some, with commitment comes the passion to bring those thoughts and ideas to life.

A friend of mine came to the U.S. from another country to go to college. After marrying she remained here rather than return to her homeland. When I met her, she seemed an outsider to American life. She dressed in a style not often seen in the U.S. Her hair covered part of her face as if she were hiding, and she often looked away when she spoke. However, she was a brilliant engineer with a firm desire to help other women in technology. Following through with that mission, she started a women's group at work.

At first, with just a handful of women attending, she was the one who had to find and introduce guests and speakers despite her insecurity. Her accent was a challenge, as was her tendency to speak softly and look anywhere but at the audience. Gradually, however, she garnered the support of other women leaders, secured needed funding, and found allies who played a crucial role in her journey. Together, they built the program into monthly hybrid (virtual and in-person) events that hundreds attended.

Over the years as she built the program, I watched her confidence grow with her passion for her cause. She even hired an image consultant to choose her wardrobe and cut her hair into a fashionable bob, but mostly she let her passion drive her. She began to choose to look up and speak out, discovering that her love for her program was contagious. The combination of enthusiastic support and a decision to grow drove her to develop a confident Leadership Presence. The key here is that she chose to seek support, and she chose to grow.

The importance of seeing Presence as a choice is that every

one of the traits described as strong, charismatic, effective Presence can be learned and developed. By exploring what affects Presence, we can make choices that better support how we want to show up.

EXERCISE

Make a video of yourself speaking for five minutes on a topic of your choice. You may want to tell a story, or talk about your work, or your upcoming vacation. Whatever it is, take a minute to get your thoughts together, but don't write them down. Don't record yourself reading. Instead, set up the phone or video camera. When you are ready, start the timer, hit record, and go! Remember that you are the only one who will hear or see this. You may hate it, but we are going to use it to increase your impact. So, just relax and be yourself.

VOCAL PRESENCE

Our voices are distinctive to us. Sure, there are regional accents, dialects, inflections that people pick up from everyday interactions, but our particular combination of all of those things is uniquely our own voice, our creation.

If you find yourself taking on the accent of a new culture or region you have been immersed in or visited, don't be alarmed. Second dialect acquisition is a well-researched phenomenon. Some people are highly susceptible to picking up dialects – convergence – while others completely deflect them – divergence. The underlying causes of second dialect acquisition are many. Some researchers believe it happens unconsciously while others say it is a matter of controlled linguistic behavior – that is, it is an empathic impulse to fit in, to reflect what we hear. Like the way we unconsciously mimic body movements of others, dialect acquisition is a way to show solidarity.

INSIGHT

For fun, try this experiment with mimicry: The next time you're in a meeting, put your hands behind your head and lean back. See how long it takes for others around the table to begin doing the same thing. People will also take drinks at the same time. This urge to synchronize with others is so powerfully contagious that we even do it during video conferences. It's part of what make us the social beings we are.

An experience I had in college taught me the power of second dialect acquisition. While a student at Pitzer College in Claremont, California, I spent a semester in an internal studies program in the Appalachian region of the U.S. Appalachia is beautiful with rolling green hills and deep crevices between the mountains that the locals call "hollers." The origin of the word is "hollow," so you can already start to see the influence of dialect.

There are tree-lined streams and thick forests except where strip mining has laid the land bare. Photographs of the Southeastern Appalachians are surprisingly reminiscent of places in the British Isles, which is precisely why the first immigrants chose to stay there. Persecuted for their

Presbyterian religion, and fleeing economic hardships, Scots-Irish settlers arrived in the mid-eighteenth century. Some moved further west, but a large group stayed in the mountains, and their rich traditions remained essentially unchanged until the coal companies entered the picture in the early 20th century.

I went to Appalachian Kentucky because of the traditional folk music, again essentially unchanged over the centuries, containing remnants or full ballads of British folk songs. In the 1960s and 70s folk music revival, artists like Joan Baez and Bob Dylan sang some of those songs, and I loved that music. I wanted to learn more about it. Unfortunately, although I tried to find places to hear it, most people there had moved on to modern country music. Moreover, I was a psychology major emphasizing Child Development, so my time was spent working with children in elementary school. As a consequence, I didn't learn much additional Appalachian folk music, but I did learn that the children could not understand a word I said when I first encountered them.

Traditionally, people in the southern U.S. speak with a "drawl," a slowed-down, drawn-out version of the American dialect. If I wanted to be understood in Kentucky, I needed to add a little Southern drawl to my California dialect. I had to learn to say "all" instead of "oil" and "char" instead of "chair" and, "I'm fixin' to go'" instead of "I am about to go." I had to linger over my words, draw out my vowels, and chew them up before they were finished. In addition to being necessary, it was fun for this grammar geek, and in the process I discovered that "y'all" (you all) is an extremely useful word, and "all y'all" is even more so.

Along with souvenirs, wonderful memories, and cherished friendships, I brought home the accent and colloquial phrases I learned from Appalachia. Even today, echoes of the Appalachian dialect creep into my conversation. I am not above telling a group of people "Okay, all ya'll. Listen up!"

If we are so susceptible to picking up dialects, if our emotions unconsciously spill over into our voice, and if others can pick up these differences in a blink of an eye and make grand inferences about who we are, where we came from, and how we are feeling, then the case for managing this is huge. Thankfully, we can indeed manage our voice.

Over the years I've spoken with many people about how I have trained voices for singing. I am always surprised when they respond with, "Well, I could never learn to be a singer because I don't have the voice for it." As someone who has spent years learning to sing and teaching others about their voices, that response is mystifying to me. With the right approach and enough practice, almost anyone can learn to be a singer or a public speaker.

The fact is, we have chosen and developed our vocal Presence from the moment we were born. Surprisingly, the muscles we use to speak were designed to help us swallow and breathe rather than to communicate. As natural as it may seem to use our voice when we speak, it took two years or more for us to learn to do that. When we began to speak, it was with our own fledgling but special creation, built by imitating the voices we heard around us. Of course, gender, size of larynx and vocal tract, genetics, geographical location, hearing, language, and cultural norms all contribute to the sound of our voices, but we are not stuck with the voice we have. With time, practice, and guidance, we can change our voice if we choose to, which, in turn, will shape our Presence.

VOCAL IMAGE

Our vocal image is the perception people get of us based on the sound of our voice. It's a mental composite of all the verbal clues others pick up about us on a subconscious level. Those bits of evidence are then reshaped by biases, beliefs, and experiences. Accents and tonal inflections, for instance, can tell a lot about where someone is from. Soft or loud volumes also say something about our emotions, mental state, or simply our hearing or lack thereof. Hesitant delivery and unsure pauses suggest a lack of confidence or an attempt at deception. Fast speakers, on the other hand, may give the impression of anxiety and undue urgency, or conversely, energy, and enthusiasm.

What is critical to note is that when our vocal habits create a vocal image that aligns to our Intention, we come across as authentic and trustworthy. When our vocal image runs counter to our Intention, the opposite happens. We may seem untrustworthy and unreliable. The case for managing our vocal image, then, is tremendous.

Studies have shown that it takes 75 percent of the body to make a single vocal sound. The interconnectedness of the body and vocal sounds is so intricate, in fact, even a sprained ankle can be heard in the voice. In 2022, researchers from the Mayo Clinic in Rochester, MN, collaborated with a researcher from the University of Tel Aviv, Israel, and demonstrated that by analyzing voice samples, artificial intelligence can predict the risk of coronary artery disease as well as its complications, such as heart attacks or chest pain.[41] Similarly, Parkinson's Disease affects the voice, and early diagnosis can lessen the impact and improve patient's living conditions. Comparison of patients' voices with machine learning models is now being used for early PD detection.[42] All of these medical conditions can affect one's vocal image.

If illness can change how a voice sounds, how might the stress of everyday life in our complex world affect it? It's common for nerves to affect people so strongly that in a difficult conversation the first words come out croaky, and they must clear their throat before continuing. Personally, I find myself constantly clearing my throat when I'm nervous, and this feeling lingers until I'm doing whatever I was stressed about. For similar reasons, singers understand the importance of opening a performance with a fun, upbeat song rather than

41   Jaskanwal, Sara, Deep Singh, et al. "Noninvasive Voice Biomarker Is Associated with Incident Coronary Artery Disease Events at Follow-up." *Mayo Clinic Proceedings, Volume 97, Issue 5*, 835 – 846. (https://www.mayoclinicproceedings.org/action/showCitFormats?doi=10.1016%2Fj.mayocp.2021.10.024&pii=S0025-6196%2821%2900808-9)
42   Ibid.

a challenging ballad, as it gives them time to overcome the effects of nerves on their voices.

Early in my career as a performing artist, I had lunch with an agent in Hollywood who spoke with a raspy voice barely above a loud whisper. When I asked him about it, he became defensive, and the lunch ended abruptly. Later, I discovered he had a condition called spasmodic dysphonia, which had developed over time, the result of the demands he felt while driving hard to succeed in the competitive entertainment industry.

Indeed, the British Voice Association has determined that emotional stress causes changes in the vocal tract resulting in changes in tone of voice. This should not be surprising since the vocal tract includes a complex nervous system, connecting to both the Central Nervous System and the Autonomic Nervous System.[43] The latter is closely linked to the emotional centers in the brain, which is why our voice changes when we get upset. This is why we recognize a change in someone else's voice when they have an emotional response to a situation. It's also why a flat tone in a voice suggests a lack of emotion, disinterest, or an absence of connection. A lack of emotion in a voice creates a perception of disinterest or disconnection, which brings me back to my point about vocal image — right or wrong, listeners get a perception of who we are based on the sound of our voices.

---

43   Harris, Sara. (2025 November 08). *"The Effects of Stress and Emotion on the Voice."* The British Voice Association. https://britishvoiceassociation.org.uk/resource/the-effects-of-stress-and-emotion-on-the-voice-3/

SHAPING VOCAL PRESENCE

We tend to have such a high regard for Leadership Presence that we fool ourselves into believing it is a natural trait which cannot be developed. You either have it or you don't. It's part of the mystique of stardom. The reality is just like so many other things in the world, it can be crafted with a fair application of attention and practice.

As we have noted, Presence should reflect Intention. If our Intention is to comfort someone who is grieving, a Presence that portrays excitement and humor may not be appropriate. Likewise, if we want to gain buy-in for a project, we should aim to project trust and confidence. In the same way that we calibrate Intention, we can also calibrate Presence so that it aligns with our Intention. To address this, we will first examine some fundamentals of shaping our vocal Presence which impact how appealing or off-putting our voices can sound to others and, respectively, how healthy or damaging they are for us.

APPEALING VOICES

On my first blog, a post I wrote called "How to Create A Sexy Voice" was among my top three posts of all time, right under "Ten Surefire Ways to Destroy Your Voice." As a side note, if you want a post to be read, it helps to use the word "sexy." My Intention with these titles was to grab attention and have some fun. Again, readers like fun, so I chose humor. My Intention for the actual content of both articles, however, was to illustrate what makes a voice appealing.

In general, people prefer voices that sound like their own.[44] Therefore, it's not unusual that our best friends probably sound a lot like us, or that international college students tend to congregate with others from their home country. But there is more. For some, pitch determines vocal attractiveness. This became evident to me some time ago when I was a member of a fundraising committee for a local charity.

The chair of the committee suffered from chronic laryngitis. This condition can last several weeks and although often painless it is characterized by a coarse hoarseness. Because of this, her voice was low and husky. Surprisingly, she would get a lot of positive reinforcement for it. To me, her voice sounded tired and unhealthy, and I worried that people would see her as lacking energy and drive because of her vocal image. One day, I took a chance and expressed my concern to her. Her reaction clearly told me she thought I was out of my mind. Chastened, I stepped away, but not before I heard someone say, "Ann, I just love listening to you. Your voice is so, well, sexy!"

Although many people, including the person who complimented my committee chair, believe a low voice is more appealing than a high voice, research findings are mixed. For example, a study by Gordon Gallup and others at the University of Albany in 2008 found that women's voices

---

44   Babel, Molly, Grant McGuire, Joseph King. "Towards a More Nuanced View of Vocal Attractiveness." PLOS ONE, 2014; 9 (2): e88616 DOI: 10.1371/journal.pone.0088616. (https://journals.plos.org/plosone/article?id=10.1371/journal.pone.0088616)

are most attractive to both men and other women when they are at the peak of fertility, which, in fact, causes their pitch to rise rather than drop. This is caused by the presence of more estrogen, just as a lower voice in men is associated with a higher level of testosterone.[45] So, let's just say the appeal of a voice may be more individual than universal.

Research has also shown that when we have an engaging conversation with someone, we tend to adjust the pitch of our own voice towards theirs — something called prosodic entrainment, harking back to our preference for similarities.[46] Families tend to gravitate toward similar pitch patterns. In my family of origin, everyone's voice was high-pitched and energetic. When I began developing my voice for singing, my voice took on a richer sound, although I am still a soprano. Even with my trained voice, I have been told that I sound just like my sister. Prosodic entrainment, therefore, can mean that we find vocal similarities attractive, especially in those we love.

Hearkening back to our discussion on regional accents, besides pitch, we judge vocal appeal by accents we hear. French often ranks high on unscientific accent preference polls by Westerners, as does British.[47] These polls indicate

45   Barras, Colin. (2025 November 08). "'Sexy' Voice Gives Fertile Women Away." New-Scientist. https://www.newscientist.com/article/mg19826544-300-sexy-voice-gives-fertile-women-away/

46   Michalsky, Jan & Schoormann, Heike & Niebuhr, Oliver. (2018). "Conversational Quality Is Affected by and Reflected in Prosodic Entrainment." 389-392. 10.21437/SpeechProsody.2018-79.

47   Baratta, Alex. (2025 November 08). "Largest-Ever Study into How People Speak Reveals the British Accent as the Most Popular Abroad." Babbel. https://uk.babbel.com/

that people link personality traits to accents, such as sophistication (British accent), and sexiness (French accent). A study conducted at the University of California Santa Cruz in 2014 found participants showed a preference for men who spoke with a shorter average word length, as well as men with a "larger" sounding voice.[48]

They also preferred women's voices that sounded "breathier" rather than "creakier." The researchers suggest this is because the former is associated with youthfulness while the latter is associated with maturity and ill health. That was true at least until people like Kim Kardashian began popularizing "vocal fry." Vocal fry is the voice's lowest register (tone), characterized by a deep, creaky, breathy sound. It's so low it is void of pitch. These studies and observations indicate that judgments people pass based on vocal appeal are complex and subjective. The question remains, does having an appealing voice give the speaker any advantage?

A Chinese study published in April 2022 explored the influence of vocal appeal on cooperative behavior in a trust game. The study hypothesized that individuals would be more willing to invest in partners with appealing voices. The behavioral results confirmed their hypothesis. The results provided evidence for the "what sounds beautiful is good" stereotype (Zuckerman and Driver, 1989). People with

press/en-gb/releases/2020-01-17-Largest-ever-study-into-how-people-speak-reveals-the-British-accen-as-the-most-popular-abroad.html
48   Babel M, McGuire G, King J (2014) "Towards a More Nuanced View of Vocal Attrac-tiveness." *PLOS ONE* 9(2): e88616. https://doi.org/10.1371/journal.pone.0088616

appealing voices were considered to have more favorable traits.[49] If a voice is healthy, the person speaking is viewed as healthy. If a voice is attractive, the person speaking is thought to be attractive as well.

 **EXERCISE**

Before going on, listen to your recording — the one you made at the beginning of this chapter. What do you hear? Do you have an accent? What is the general pitch of your voice? Describe the tone. What do others hear when they hear you speak?

CREATING RESONANCE AND BREATHING

We may associate a strong Presence with a powerful and attractive voice, but that kind of voice is not always innate. Moreover, it cannot be attributed solely to the shape or size of the person or how loudly or pleasingly they talk.

As a voice practitioner and singer, I've learned that one thing that makes a voice pleasing and powerful is a specific kind of resonance. This is called "mask resonance." Mask resonance is a forward placement of sound that can be formed by combining the bright, edginess of nasal resonance with mouth resonance. It is present to some degree in all vocal sounds since we open our mouths to speak and sing,

49   Shang Junchen, Liu Zhihui. "Vocal Attractiveness Matters: Social Preferences in Cooperative Behavior." *Frontiers in Psychology*. Volume 13 – 2022. DOI=10.3389/fpsyg.2022.877530   URL=https://www.frontiersin.org/journals/psychology/articles/10.3389/fpsyg.2022.877530

but it can be developed to a greater extent with exercises and training. It clearly gives the speaker an advantage.

A voice with plenty of mask resonance is strong and clear, no matter how loud or soft. A voice with good mask resonance is pleasant to listen to, vibrant and flexible, and rich in vocal variety. However, intensifying mask resonance by design is not something we do naturally. In fact, the "natural" voice is a misnomer since using our voices to communicate is something we must learn. Most mammals are born with the ability to communicate effectively with their own species, but humans are not. Humans learn to communicate with each other through imitation and trial and error.

The study of different kinds of resonance for varied vocal effects in singing began in Italy with the rise of Bel Canto singing back in the 16th century and had a revival in the late 20th century. Bel Canto, or beautiful singing, is a style focused on communicating different emotions with distinct tones and vocal colors, with those colors and tones being suggested by the qualities inherent to four unique kinds of vocal resonance – chest, mouth, head, and mask. The different kinds of resonance roughly correspond with the different physical areas in which sound resonates and is felt once it leaves the vocal folds.

Head resonance is soft and sweet, chest resonance is dark and adds a sense of gravity and drama to a voice, mouth resonance is more conversational in character. The beauty of mask resonance is that it involves mouth resonance as well as

 **EXERCISE**

If you want to develop mask resonance to strengthen your speaking voice and modify your Presence by changing your vocal image, throw your ego to the wind and get ready to make some funny sounds:

Find it in your face. Say "Mmmmm" or "Mmm-hmm." See if you can feel the buzzy sensation in the front of your face. Now say, "Mmm-hmm one. Mmm-hmm two. Mmm-hmm three." Can you feel that sensation carry over into the words "one," "two" and "three?" If you can't, then work to produce those words in the same resonance by making more of a cartoony voice. Then relax into your natural voice, while holding onto the vibrations you feel in the front of your face.

Practice. Use mask resonance at the beginning of a sentence and see if you can keep that sensation in the words that follow. For example, say, "Mmmmmm. It's great to see you." Did you feel the resonance in the mask as you said, "It's great to see you," or did it fade away? Try it again. Start by practicing this five minutes a day and then work up to 20 minutes a day.

nasal resonance which creates a clear, articulate sound. It also helps us turn up the volume.

Along with mask resonance, breathing is important to our vocal image. Obviously, breathing is also important for our health and well-being. Good respiratory function allows us to filter the air we take in, distribute oxygen to the body, and eliminate carbon dioxide. When we breathe deeply and use our breath to project our words, we project a Presence of strength because we are calmer and more grounded, more oxygenated. Again, vocal fitness follows overall fitness. The healthier we are, the healthier our voice will be.

Singing teachers often say that breathing is the key to great singing. This stems from the Bel Canto again which focused on Appoggio, a special kind of breathing. However, although people have tried to figure out what Appoggio was or is, the exact technique is hazy. Today, there are many breathing techniques for singing, speaking, meditation, and exercising that can be found online.

As mentioned earlier, a post I wrote for Valentine's Day about sexy voices has been an ongoing hit. I was even interviewed about it several times. The big surprise for the radio hosts was discovering the exercises most helpful to creating a sexy voice involve making some bizarre sounds, which is not what one usually recommends on Valentine's Day. Frankly, all vocal exercises will sound odd at first, but as I've told many people, most of us don't do push-ups to look good doing push-ups. Similarly, we do vocal exercises to improve our voices rather than to sound beautiful vocalizing.

If we truly want to develop a good vocal image, we can start by reflecting on what our Intention is. Keeping our Intention in mind will help us to create the right vocal image to support it. Second, try some daily vocal exercises. Get physical. By creating a routine for exercising our voice we develop muscle memory and healthy vocal habits. Third, when the opportunities avail we should take the chance to get up in front of others and express ourselves with conviction.

VOCAL DETRACTORS

On the flip side of what makes voices appealing are habits people have that take away from their vocal image. Some vocal detractors are due to poor enunciation, such as lazy articulation and slurred words. Some are due to too much vocal tension, including grunts and squeaks or over-compressed (squeezed) voices. A breathy or flat voice, for example, may result from too little tension at the vocal fold level. Habits, such as lip smacking, tongue clicking, and noisy breathing, are often created unawares perhaps because of anxiety. Detractors are rarely used on purpose. Thankfully, there are techniques we can learn to minimize them.

It should be noted that there are vocal detractors caused by debilitating physical conditions. While these are beyond the scope of this book, I have included a list of resources at the end of the book, and a note about how to find the help you need.

Although I have heard many vocal detractors over time, let's look at three of the most common ones to better understand the effect unconscious habits can have on vocal image and how we are perceived.

DROPPING WORDS

One of the most common and unproductive vocal habits

I hear is speakers dropping the volume of their last words to an almost inaudible level. I'm convinced the habit is a result of people being hunched over their computers all day, speaking into headsets rather than across rooms. Headset microphones can pick up and amplify sounds for intimate conversations, and speakers get used to that. Over time, they create an overreliance on artificial amplification and people fall into bad vocal habits.

Other times speakers just run out of air. If we haven't practiced what we are going to say, or if we're exploring a new idea, we may misjudge the amount of air and energy needed to completely vocalize an idea because we haven't fully thought the idea out. In simple terms, we don't have enough runway to get our ideas off the ground. We end up swallowing the final words of a sentence. Those final words often carry the entire point of our message.

Unfortunately, dropping words at the end of sentences produces a vocal image of someone lacking energy, clarity, and confidence. When it becomes habitual, that vocal image then becomes our vocal reputation or brand. I don't think anyone wants to be known for a lack of energy, clarity, and confidence. There is, however, a way to think about speaking that can help change the habit of dropping words and create a bigger Presence and it can be found using the word "WOW."

When speakers need to be heard by a large audience in a large venue, the space of the room demands space in the voice, just like the word "WOW." Slower pace, pausing, elongating vowel sounds, and cranking up the volume are vocal characteristics that create space. Vowel sounds in English are voiced sounds. That is, the vocal folds vibrate and make audible vibrations when we say "I, E, A, O, and U." "Wow" creates vocal space because we automatically emphasize the vowel sound, and once we feel that space, we can duplicate the feeling in the last words in a sentence, lean into the vowels and increase our Presence all the way through to the end of a talk.

Rather than save the vocal space for special presentations, I recommend using it all the time, particularly if you are in the habit of dropping the ends of your sentences. Just as the word "WOW" conjures up images of big things, the vocal space used to create it also creates an image of someone who is excited and has important things to say. It is the sound of someone who is not concerned that they will be interrupted. They command the conversation.

UPSPEAK

Just as voiced vowel sounds improve our delivery and therefore our Presence, conscious use of intonation adds value as well. Inflection caused by vocal pitch has a definite effect, meaning we can deliberately shift inflection to correspond with the message we are conveying. There are some types of inflection that people tend to use that may also act as vocal detractors.

One detractor that has become popular in recent years

 **EXERCISE**

Pull out the recording that you made earlier. If you skipped that exercise, make a recording now. Then listen to it. Do you drop your voice at the end of sentences? If so, how does that affect your vocal image? Now, try saying, "WOW." What happens when you say it? Can you duplicate that feeling in other words by slowing down, accentuating the vowels and breathing energy into your words? Try it first and after some trials, record yourself again. Apply what you've learned to the new recording and compare this one to the first.

is called "upspeak." Linguists describe it as a rising terminal. From a musical perspective it is an open cadence. Simply put, it is created by raising the pitch at the end of a sentence. In English, this rising intonation indicates an invitation for an answer and is primarily used to ask a yes or no question such as "Do we have a meeting today?"

Besides asking a question, the rising terminal may be used to invite people into a conversation. The intonation creates space for others to add their views. We do this automatically as a form of relational communication. However, the drawback with too much upspeak in meetings, speeches, and important conversations is that it diminishes the power of what we say by causing us to sound indecisive. Upspeak has become so pervasive that some people turn almost every statement into a question, causing slam poet and teacher Taylor Mali to observe: "In case you hadn't noticed, it has somehow become uncool to sound like you know what you're talking about?"[50]

To make a statement in English, we usually bring the voice down in pitch. Right? (That's another way we sound indecisive — follow a statement with a question looking for agreement.) However, no matter how bold statements are in English, if we intone them as questions, people see us as unable to commit to our ideas. But wouldn't the converse be true? Could we use too much down-speak (descending terminal, or closed cadence?) The answer is a definitive "yes." Too much declamatory speech creates a vocal image of someone who is uncompromising, strict, or rigid.

The point is, ending sentences consistently with only open or closed cadence is boring and can convey perceptions you may not want others to take away. The best use of cadence is a conscious mix of upspeak and downspeak. Make definitive statements, but also ask questions and invite response.

 **EXERCISE**

Pull out the recording that you made earlier. If you skipped that exercise, make a recording now. Then listen to it. Do you raise your pitch at the end of sentences? If so, how does that affect your vocal image? If you can't decide what you are hearing, listen for upspeak and down speak in on-line examples. Then, experiment with upspeak and downspeak. After some trials, record yourself again. Apply what you've learned to the new recording and compare this one to the first.

50   Mali, Taylor. (2025 November 08). *"Totally like whatever, you know?"* TaylorMali. https://taylormali.com/poems/totally-like-whatever-you-know/

How we end a sentence involves using inflection; inflection is primarily caused by a change in vocal pitch or tone color. Some people hear pitch better than others. However, inflection can also be tied to Intention and that can be useful when learning to use more vocal variety. A great way to gain a better understanding of how inflection works to create meaning is to say the word "oh" in response to different prompts and listen for how it sounds each time. The prompts are:

1. Say the word "oh" like you are sad.
2. Say the word "oh" like you are happy.
3. Say the word "oh" like you are disappointed.
4. Say the word "oh" like you are angry.
5. Say the word "oh" like you are mistaken.
6. Say the word "oh" like you have been forgotten.
7. Say the word "oh" like you are the happiest person alive. And so forth.

Recording one's responses can be even more helpful, especially if you listen to what you've recorded.

FILLER WORDS

Improving one's Presence requires effort. Improving some vocal habits comes more naturally than others, like breathing. Since we must do it repeatedly to survive, we are frequently reminded to turn our attention to it, making behavioral change easier. Others will take a lifetime of diligence. One of the pesky vocal habits that takes time and effort to eliminate is the use of empty words and phrases. We all use them to one degree or another and the more we do, the more they diminish our Presence. Examples are "kind of," "sort of," "um," "you know," and "like." Linguists call these words "hesitation markers" since they are often used to fill the gaps when we don't know what to say.

To write clearly and concisely, professional writers try to avoid "empty qualifiers" such as "really" and "very." The benefit writing has over speaking is when we write we typically have more time to polish what is being communicated. When speaking, we are immediately present and there is no time to revise!

I have a friend who conducts interviews with musicians and bands. He loves it except for one excruciating step in the process: After he records the interviews on video and uses software to transcribe the audio files to text, he then edits the text before producing the interviews in written format. It seems easy enough, but the editing reveals a terrible truth about himself, one he must face every time he does an interview. The transcription includes every repeated word, every use of "like," "kind of," and "you know," stark reminders that empty words and phrases riddle his spoken word. On the positive side, this has given him a major incentive to learn to eliminate empty words when he speaks!

He shouldn't be so hard on himself. The average person uses filler words five or more times per minute. When I hear people using fillers so much that it is distracting, I set my timer and start counting. Even in some politicians' speeches I have heard as many as 20 fillers per minute. However, if we completely eliminate fillers, we run the risk of sounding unnatural.

Perhaps more surprising, psycholinguistic researchers have discovered that "um" and "uh" may have a different use than other hesitation markers — it's been observed that as a person's socio-economic status go up, so does the prevalence of "um's'" and "uh's."[51] Studying this more closely, researchers

---

 **EXERCISE**

How many minutes is the recording you made at the beginning of this chapter? Count the fillers you hear and determine your average usage. If you have more than 1-4 per minute, it's time to eliminate some of them.

Step 1 - Pick one – the one you use the most – set a timer for one minute and begin speaking while concentrating on not using that filler word. Do this once a day for a week.

Step 2 - Try it out in the real world. For the next week, pick one conversation a day in which you will concentrate on not using that filler. Make it a low-stakes conversation such as lunch with a good friend.

Step 3 - It takes about 21 days to create a new habit, so keep up daily practicing and after you've minimized your use of one filler, work on another. At some point it may drive you crazy to even think about filler words, but you are well on your way to reducing them. Keep going!

---

51   Fridland, Valerie M. (2025 November 08). "Presidential Pauses? What Those 'Ums' and 'Uhs' Really Tell Us About Candidates for the White House." *The Conversation.* https://theconversation.com/presidential-pauses-what-those-ums-and-uhs-really-tell-us-about-candidates-for-the-white-house-204972

feel the vocalized pauses are a signal that we are about to say something complex, a way of either alerting the listener to pay attention or allowing the speaker time to consider the best way to say what they have to say.

Of course, even though there may be constructive use for empty words, the overuse of them can be annoying. So, is there a perfect not-so-perfect habit for adding words that do not add any meaning to what we are saying? The answer is yes. One to four filler words per minute is optimal for sounding natural, retaining audience attention, and conveying messages effectively.

Although we might sound too studied if we eliminate them completely, anyone who has tried to clean up their speech of empty words will say it's not easy to break the habit. However, there is a time-tested way to reduce our reliance on hesitation markers. Since nerves are one of the biggest reasons people overuse vocal fillers, one of the cures can be

 **EXERCISE**

Once aware, we can often get rid of a filler before we say it. To practice this technique, pick a topic to speak about. Set a timer for 2 minutes and begin talking. When you feel yourself about to use a filler/hesitation marker, stop and say nothing for enough time to snap your fingers or tap your pen once on a desk. Then continue. If you feel another filler start to creep in, stop and pause in the same way as before. Add this technique to your daily practice sessions for a week. During the following week, allow silence or take a breath instead of either fillers or finger snaps.

found by practicing speeches or presentations beforehand. Yep, more groundbreaking news! Practice helps. In this case it is because the more comfortable we are with what we plan to say, the less hesitation we feel when we say it.

I say *one* of the cures is practice because practice is probably the easiest to apply. However, the reason we use filler words is to give ourselves time to think about what to say next, to look for the perfect word and to breathe. Sound familiar? That's right, we use filler words for the same purpose we should be using pauses. Not surprisingly, one of the cures for using too many empty words is to use pauses instead.

THE SOUND OF SILENCE

One of the most powerful shapers of vocal Presence is one that is defined by the absence of voice. Silence. Silence can have both negative and positive effects depending on when and how it occurs. For the most part, if we use it deliberately, we have a high chance of using it for good.

Way back in 1966, Simon and Garfunkel released their seminal album *Sounds of Silence*. On that album is the song, "The Sound of Silence." Art Garfunkel has said it is essentially about "the inability of people to communicate with each other, not particularly internationally but especially emotionally, so what you see around you are people unable to love each other."[52] In late 2015, the heavy metal group Disturbed covered the song. Their version underscores that

---

52   Eliot, Marc. *Paul Simon: A Life*. John Wiley and Sons, 2010.

theme of detachment through its contrasting vocal styles. After listening to either version, we are struck with just how loud silence can be.

Perhaps it's because of this power that we are often afraid to let silence creep into a conversation or, much worse, a presentation. Many people have the misconception that pausing while speaking is a bad thing. Maybe we're afraid we'll forget where we are in our thoughts, or that someone else will jump in before we can finish our idea. Either might happen but that doesn't make silence less important.

Contrary to popular belief, pausing is not a sign of weakness. Pausing gives others space to take in what has been said. It's natural. On stage, actors use pauses and silence to add emphasis to poignant ideas. And a pause doesn't have to be long to be effective. Most pauses are what actors call "a beat," or the equivalent of how long it takes to snap our fingers once.

Research shows that most conversational speech consists of short (0.20 seconds), medium (0.60 seconds), and long (over one second) pauses. Great public speakers often pause for two to three seconds or even longer. Data collected by the research firm Quantified Communications shows that the average speaker only uses 3.5 pauses per minute,[53] and considering they may use more than five filler words, replacing fillers with pauses provides a less irritating balance.

Another benefit to pausing is that it gives us time to

---

53   Zandran, Noah. "How to Stop Saying 'Um,' 'Ah,' and 'You Know." *Harvard Business Review.* August 01, 2018.

breathe. If we don't pause when speaking, we risk running out of air. This will result in lowering our volume, losing energy, and swallowing the last words of our sentences. The ultimate consequence, of course, is losing our audience's interest and confidence. Ironically, professional speakers deliberately use pauses to help them be heard by large audiences in large spaces. Thinking back to the "WOW" concept, we know that the space of a large room or hall demands large space in the voice. Pausing, along with slower pace, elongated vowel sounds., and increased volume. are vocal characteristics that create space.

The most important benefit of choosing to use pauses is that it grounds us and the audience. It not only gives an audience time to take in what we have said, it gives us time to consider the impact our words and ideas are having on the audience, it gives us a moment to consider our next sentence, and it gives us time to expand. In other words, the sound of silence is not something to be afraid of. Rather, when used consciously, silence can have a positive effect on our Presence.

 **EXERCISE**

At some point you may want to record another version of the talk you did at the opening of this chapter. This time, consciously eliminate filler words by pausing and consider planning for silence. Where else would silence be useful to make a point or allow time for the audience to take in what you've said?

AWARENESS AND PRESENCE

We are at the mercy of the unconscious unless we become aware of our habits, vocal or otherwise. We create an impression even if we are ignorant of what that impression is. When I was in high school, one of my teachers had a habit of making little grunting sounds whenever there was silence in the room for an extended period of time, such as when we were taking a test.

Her small round physique aligned perfectly with the impression she gave with her involuntary sounds, which is how she earned the derogatory nickname of "Little Piggy." Of course, young people can be cruel, but I am also sure she had no idea she was making those sounds. Awareness would have increased her ability to change her behavior, bolstered her image, making it more likely for others to see her as the intelligent, skillful teacher she was.

It can be useful to start to pay attention to vocal detractors, but it's also helpful to listen for what is absent from a voice. One of the top turn-offs for an audience is a monotone voice or the lack of expression. This can be linked to many things, including the simple fact that some people just don't hear pitch. Or, as we often see in business, a speaker's connection to the topic is less emotional than is needed to engage an audience. Or maybe it is, but daily review of the information or giving the same talk repeatedly can contribute to a loss of interest for both the presenter and the audience. The need to engage, however, is critical when facing an organization to drive action or when speaking to sell our ideas.

I've heard businesspeople say they are uncomfortable with expressive speaking. For some, sounding "emotional" is not appropriate for a business presentation. Others have told me it doesn't sound natural to them. What I know is that inflection begins to show up effortlessly when people are passionate about their topic or when they tell a story, demonstrating that it is a natural process. I have yet to hear anyone who is incapable of being expressive with their voice when telling a meaningful personal story. As with other vocal habits, learning to listen and becoming aware of the voice we have created is critical to finding or re-finding our authentic voices.

Just as people may not always be aware of intonation or the lack of it in a voice, they may not always be aware of what the rest of their body is saying when they present or deliver a speech. I watched one very attractive woman give a talk in a workshop and noticed that her right hand kept rising in front of her for no particular reason. Not only did it rise up, but her fingers would start to curl until it looked like she was imitating the claw of a large bird. Of course, the gesture was distracting and seemed incongruent with how she looked, so, I asked her if she knew she was doing it. Her answer was, "No."

Unfortunately, in a workshop there is not enough time to completely change behavior so what we try to do is create awareness, knowing that awareness is the first step toward change. In this case, every time she raised her hand, I brought the move to her attention, and by the end of the day, she had stopped doing it. But with one problem temporarily solved, another arose. In her final presentation of the day, she was in front of the group of her peers when she stopped suddenly and said softly, "I think I am just weird. I do weird things with my hands; my sense of humor is odd, and I sound weird. I'm quirky."

She felt vulnerable and exposed, so much so that she couldn't continue. I took a moment, leaned into her, and said, "So, be quirky if it's the real you." As she finished her talk, she relaxed a bit and gave herself permission to use the humor that bubbled up naturally from her unique observations. We all enjoyed it, chuckled, and never once felt it was inappropriate.

Years later she told me accepting her quirkiness was a

 **INSIGHT**

Since the entertainment industry is so prevalent and influential on our daily lives, it's not unreasonable to look at the actor's tool kit to find a way to develop more expression. What we discover is a way to increase vocal variety even when we're not feeling it. Actors use a technique called "emotional recall" to bring up their personal experience and help create emotion in their voices. It involves recalling a personal memory of a situation like the one they are portraying as their character. The objective is to import the feelings from those memories into their performance. Emotional recall is something anyone can use to bring more meaning into their communication.

pivotal point in her career. "It is who I am. I can try not to do it because it might not seem professional but it's who I am and if I actually let myself be who I am, I have a lot more brainpower and thought focus to put into the real work, not just into public speaking."

PRESENCE IN THE BODY

Although strengthening vocal image by building healthy vocal habits will go a long way toward establishing a desired Presence, we can add to that growth by becoming aware of body language. How we use our hands and arms, and how that aligns with the impression others have of us also affects Presence. Since body language and spoken language are intricately linked in the brain, they are critical to Presence when applied to our impact as communicators. So, let's consider how posture, gestures of all types, and body language can affect the perception other people have of us and even the perception we have of ourselves.

Vocalists, from classically-trained opera singers to heavy metal belters, know that how they stand on the stage, how they move, and even how they position their arms will dramatically impact what happens with their voice. If you don't believe this, watch a video of Pretty Yende performing live or, if your tastes run more visceral, try Bruce Dickenson from Iron Maiden. For more moderate palates, maybe Freddie Mercury from Queen. Or to really mix it up, you can watch opera star Monserrat Caballé perform with Freddie Mercury singing "Barcelona" to a roaring crowd.

Whichever music or performer you prefer, take note of how they use their posture and gestures to affect their sound. Watch how they open their stances wide and crouch just a bit to engage their cores, looking as if they are pulling the energy up from the stage, into their feet, then their legs to gain more vocal power, watch how they open their chests and throw their arms up to broaden the space they occupy. They have intimate knowledge of what happens to their voice when they sit, stand, or walk.

As you watch you may notice that these actions do two things: They impact the body's ability to draw breath, energy, and power and to propel it through voice. They also, through the poetry of motion, convey thought and feeling, and the better the two are connected the more stirring the performance.

A careful observer may see how these performers bring Intention and Presence together to deliver brilliant artistry. And just as these performers convey their Intention through their stage Presence and vocal projection, so do we every time we walk into a room and do something as simple as engage in mild conversation. Indeed, all the world is a stage.

I remember the first time I saw my husband walk on stage. It was at a conference where he introduced Martin Short to a large crowd. At the time, he was the Chief Marketing Officer of the tech company hosting the event and it was a triumph to have signed up Mr. Short for an interview. I was in the audience that day, excited to see my guy up there, but I noticed that he seemed uncomfortable. Instead of confidently greeting the audience, he kept his head down and mumbled into his mic. Even during the interview, he avoided making eye contact with the audience.

Martin Short, being a professional, handled the interview well, and the audience cheered enthusiastically when it was over. Later that day, we talked, and it was surprising to learn that some people don't enjoy being on stage. I also learned that there's a difference between wanting to captivate an audience and hoping to get off the stage as soon as possible – when it comes to Presence, what you think matters. Overcoming nerves is difficult, but while Martin Short probably focuses on what he brings to an audience, my husband was focused on being judged. Focusing on what other people think is the surest path to stage fright reflected in a Presence that lacks confidence.

Physical Presence isn't just limited to walking on a stage or into a meeting room. We also make an impression when we show up in a virtual meeting or create a video on our phones. First, we are either present or not depending on whether or not we turn on our camera in a virtual meeting. Second, we have choices we can make about our background and our filters. As I get older, I find that I like the "soft focus" filters more. However, I'm not a fan of backgrounds that obscure my hair or part of my head. Presence is important, and I don't want to seem partially present.

A background can make or break Presence. I used to have virtual coaching sessions with a client every Friday. We'd start by celebrating the end of the week, but deep down, we were both itching to kick off the weekend. To stay focused, I decided to embrace the weekend vibes. I found a background image of a Starbucks in Cayucos, California, and set it as my virtual setting. When the meeting started, my client burst out laughing and said she loved the idea of taking our Friday sessions out of the office. And because I've never really liked having meetings on Friday afternoons, it may seem silly, but I was more content, too.

So, how we think about ourselves and walk through our lives shows up in our bodies. It affects how we carry ourselves, whether or not we look at others, and, therefore, the impression we make on others. We are often at the mercy of our subconscious mind, but once we become more aware we are more in control of our choices. In that way, we become more in control of how others perceive us.

SMALL GESTURES

One of the most fascinating aspects to watch when someone speaks is their gestures. Many people suggest that "speaking with your hands" is a habit specific to one's culture, but I have seen people of all cultures use gestures liberally. I should also note that while some gestures occur subconsciously, others are more calculated. Gestures can be useful to convey energy levels, to illustrate points, and to direct focus. Many people have favorite gestures that they rely on to emphasize points or underscore key concepts. In fact, without awareness, many people have odd, repetitive gestures that speak more of nerves than their topic. It's also true that gestures are a form of paralanguage, and as such will say a lot about what we are thinking or feeling.

The trick, of course, is to ensure our gestures align with our message and with our Intention. Below are a few situations and the gestures we may see. It can be useful to think about how and when we have seen gestures in practice and also to think about how we use them ourselves. Although it can be frightening, it can also be useful to ask a friend to make a video during a conversation so that we can get a peek at how others see us when it comes to our body language.

What we do with our hands can be illuminating. I've seen businesspeople get up on stage to speak to their organizations all the while clenching their fists and pointing index fingers at the crowd. I've seen others open their arms as if to embrace the audience. Still others may extend their arms in the same way they would if offering to shake hands with the people in the first row. Each gesture tells the audience something about the speaker. Pointing is accusative. Open arms are inviting. Handshakes are cordial. When a speaker uses motivating words but points accusatively, she sends a mixed message that affects her impact.

Folded arms say, "I'm closed or I'm cold." Praying hands express gratitude. If someone asks me if I speak Spanish, I often respond by holding up my forefinger and thumb as if I am pinching an object about an inch in diameter and saying, *"un pequeño,"* which is "just a little" in Spanish. If I want someone to halt what they are doing or saying, I may hold up my hand with my palm facing them.

Although we may think all gestures are universal. In the U.S., we see a head shake, a gesture in which the head is turned left and right along the transverse plane repeatedly in quick succession, as a negative gesture. It's a "no" to us, but surprisingly, in some parts of the world, most notably Bulgaria and some areas of Eastern Europe, the opposite is true. There, a vehement head shake means "yes!"

GRAND GESTURES

There are also larger, full- or half-body gestures. As one might expect, these gestures are made not with hands, but with our entire bodies. These gestures tend to captivate the audience and can sometimes seem like a dance. The amazing thing is how well they convey meaning and add volume to messages.

One example is the "us and them" gesture, or "this and that." With this gesture we square our hands in front of us as if we are holding a box between them. We may even jolt our hands to give a sense of immediacy as if to say: "In this spot we have xyz." We then take a few steps to the side and make the gesture again. "While over here we have abc." This gesture helps to underscore the passing of time, linear progression, or differentiate between two ideas or entities.

Another large gesture is the clean sweep motion. With this gesture we make a sweeping motion with one arm as if swiping everything off a desk. This gesture conveys the idea of moving past things or issues, as if we are removing obstacles and starting with a "clean slate."

A colleague of mine used to favor the phrase, "capture that." Often when he felt he had made a clear point and wanted to move to the next point in his discussion, he would say, "Capture that." He would then make a gesture as if he had picked up an object from a table in front of him and placed it to his side. When he did this, you really felt like he had literally captured the idea. It was as if he was saying, "Okay, we agreed on this item. Now let's put it over here so it won't get lost."

Sometimes we don't need to move our bodies at all to make grand or full body gestures. Where and how we sit in a room can be indicative of our interests. As an example, the direction our feet point is the direction we want to go, and if they point to the door when we are in a meeting, that's a pretty good indication we'd rather be somewhere else. The same is true when we are standing in conversation. The next time you have a chat with a colleague, pay attention to where your feet are pointing. Are your feet saying you'd like to have a nice, engaging discussion or that you'd rather be elsewhere?

Gestures, small and large, are fun and once we tune in to them, it's easy to see how they speak loudly about what we are thinking. It's surprising to learn how many we use on a regular basis without even realizing it. Through observation and a little research, we can discover what our gestures are saying to others about our Presence and decide if we are creating the perception we want with them.

SYMBOLIC GESTURES

Conscious use of gestures can bolster our projected confidence as well as our self-confidence. As Anna sings in the American musical, *The King and I*, "When you fool the people you fear, you fool yourself as well." But gestures do not always have to be hand or body movements. Gestures can also be symbols or road signs to others and even to ourselves about our Intention. A friend of mine says that when he wants to bolster his confidence at work, he'll throw on a blazer that he keeps handy in his office. Not only does it help keep him warm in the freezing temperatures of his office building, but it gives him a sense of reassurance which, in turn, helps him to be more comfortable and to project conviction.

We all know that we shouldn't judge a book by its cover and that assumptions often lead to false stereotypes. The reality is, however, it's common in most cultures to perceive a smartly dressed person as well organized and, conversely, a slovenly dressed person as careless. This is especially true in workplaces where dress codes are enforced. Of course, both conjectures can quickly prove false through observable actions and behaviors, but it is also true that what we wear and how we hold ourselves can influence how we feel about ourselves.

It was during my experience of going through a divorce that my belief in "you are what you wear" was validated by a temporary tattoo. I had to attend a custody hearing to determine how our children would be affected by our split. A divorce in and of itself is difficult. Factor in children and it becomes exponentially more stressful. A mother always wants to protect her child. From my experience, knowing how much a divorce can hurt them makes it feel as if you are physically and personally inflicting pain upon them. It's a terrible feeling. As a consequence, I was feeling stressed. My confidence was shaky as I got dressed that morning and it was at that moment that I remembered the tattoo.

Someone had given my four-year-old a set of temporary tattoos, one of which was a picture of a beautiful but slightly terrifying wolf. Hoping my daughter wouldn't miss it, and thinking it wasn't really the best choice for a four-year-old anyway, I quickly found the tattoo, applied it to my chest where no one would see its ferocious, mama-wolf teeth. No one but me would know it was there, but as I finished dressing, though it may seem odd, my spirits were suddenly elevated. I even smiled a little as I walked out the door. I was no longer the helpless lamb before the slaughter of the courthouse and an overly complicated bureaucratic system, I was the mama-wolf, a fierce protector of her pups, a fighter, a survivor.

The outcome was as positive as one might expect. There were more court dates, more papers to be filed, more statements to be signed, but through it all, I kept my head up. Even though the tattoo faded, I kept that image and spirit in mind and close to heart. It made a difference.

PRESENCE IN THE ENVIRONMENT

Dolores was a small, young woman, fresh out of college with big ambitions in a new job. She was part of a mostly male team. When she spoke, her voice was high and soft, and though her youthful vigor was charming, her ideas often got lost among the louder voices of her peers.

One of her male colleagues who sat near her in meetings loved her ideas. He valued them so much that he repeated what she said so it could be heard by others. But he also claimed them as his own. She tried speaking as loudly as possible, but when she did, her voice rose in pitch until the exertion tickled her throat and made her cough. She tried holding up her hand but that felt more like grade school and only served to reinforce the image of her as a young girl.

Over time, her conviction that she had found the right path was waning and every night she crawled into bed, pulled the covers over her head, and prayed for an answer or a new job. She was a dynamic young woman with bottomless creativity who desired to move up in the organization. However, as with so many petite, young women, she seemed to get lost in the crowd of high-potential emerging leaders. Her boss, who was a client of mine, believed she had a tremendous amount of talent and wanted to see her succeed. He suggested she work with me, and I was happy to help.

To begin, we discussed her Intention as well as her environment. What we discovered was that Dolores didn't just want to be heard vocally. This wasn't about turning up the volume of her voice. She wanted to be noticed and to have her ideas and contributions heard and acknowledged. I knew it would help to enhance her voice, because Dolores could create a richer sound that carried better. However, if the problem was being a young woman in a sea of men, she was never going to sound like a man. And she didn't want to.

In addition to improving her voice, we decided that she could use a little disruption. We came up with a plan: she could increase her Presence further by changing the environment in which she appeared.

At the next opportunity, she arrived at the meeting a little early. Sitting in her chair, she placed her laptop so that it slightly encroached on the space of the person who would sit in the chair next to hers (a space usually belonging to that man who loved her ideas). She did the same on the opposite side with her water bottle, and directly in front of her she set a notepad and pen. She spread out a couple of books in the empty spaces around the notepad, and laid her phone, a little beyond the last gap at the top of her table area, face down.

Finally, she put her forearms on the table with her elbows extended out away from her body. If nothing else, the space she now occupied felt more significant, and though no one remarked on how she had spread out, when she had something to say, she felt so much more confident that she rose slightly out of her chair and leaned forward into the conversation. And it worked. After the discussion, she gathered her newfound self-reliance, taking it with her to the next meeting and the next.

Over time, Dolores' gestures have become more expansive and more open, and she leans into the meeting rather than settling in, slumped in her chair. Her voice is stronger, but she has also developed a bold, strong attitude so now others can't help but sense her Presence despite her small stature.

 **INSIGHT**

If you have a soft voice or the room muffles your sound you can increase your volume by using the hard surfaces around you to amplify the sound. One of the best ways to do this is to speak into a corner so the sound bounces back to all. In a similar way to how one should try out the sound on their computer before entering a ZOOM meeting, always try out the sound in a room before speaking if you need to be heard.

A friend of mine is an avid photographer. She always has been. There was a time when she would cart her expensive camera around with her everywhere we went. Over the last many years though, I have become something of a photo taker as well. I don't have a super nice camera, like my friend, but I do have a good phone, and I have learned how to use various filters and features. These help to sharpen my images and highlight aspects of the picture that I want to emphasize. Improving Presence is like this. It sharpens our image, clarifies our ideas, and helps people we communicate with better understand what we are saying. As I've repeated, it takes awareness and practice to work with our Intention and Presence. There also comes a time when we must apply what we've learned – put it out there in the world and see what happens. And when we do, we may find that the controlled environment of our office or conference room is not at all like the environments that test our Presence the most.

PRESENCE IN THE AGE OF VIDEO CONFERENCING

Back in 2001, people were already using conference call technology to conduct meetings, particularly those in the tech sector, and although pervasive video technology was still a distant threat, people could be as absent then as they are today.

One day I was on one of those calls, waiting for a few more people to dial in, and we suddenly heard what sounded like heavy breathing on the line. Someone had forgotten to mute their cell phone while they were listening. Immediately, the jokes started. The sexual implications were top of mind and implied, but people also suggested the person might be jogging, or walking out to get the mail, or cleaning the house. Thirteen years later, the conference call company Intercall published research from interviews with over 500 Americans and determined that people do unanticipated things while on mute. Intercall found:

- 82% of people were likely to do something unrelated while on a conference call, such as email or even chasing their dog down the street.[54]
- Women were likely to mute a call to shop online while men were more likely to use the restroom while on mute.

Today, most of us know that using video has not helped the situation much. People are still not engaged. Even with great cameras, the emotional elements and stimuli are not present in most conference calls. When people are on mute, their immediate response to the speaker's humor is missing. When people turn off their video cameras and are not on the screen, their facial expressions are no longer visible. And when we only see slides, we don't get a sense of connection with the other humans on the call.

Another aspect of video is the expectation that we can use it without training. I received a request to work with a senior executive at one of the world's most influential companies. His seniority was hard to believe when I saw him on the video. He spoke so fast I could barely understand him and the rhythm

---

54   Gavett, Gretchen. (2025 November 08). "What People Are Really Doing When They're on a Conference Call." *Harvard Business Review*. https://hbr.org/2014/08/what-people-are-really-doing-when-theyre-on-a-conference-call

and slur of his slick, used-car-salesman speech pattern paired with his off-beat lime-green jacket seemed to contradict his title as a senior vice president.

I was intrigued. A challenge indeed. How on earth was it possible for this man to be in his position? Was he extraordinarily smart, or was there something I was missing? Soon after, I was in the lobby of the Executive Briefing Center waiting to meet the awkward gentleman. I had time to ponder the situation, and my curiosity was brimming, but I was not naïve either. People like him want Executive Presence, but it is hard work to guide them to find it. They can't hear themselves and can't see how others perceive them, so they are rarely able to modify their behavior.

The glass door swung open and in strode a statuesque man with a gracious smile, dressed impeccably in an expensive, dark navy suit. His charm was infectious as I watched him acknowledge others with a nod or a powerful handshake. It was as if he were friends with everyone in the room. He exuded confidence and magnetism. Imagine my surprise when I learned that this confident, classy executive was the gawky man in the video, and my new client.

Although there was no question that vocal image played a part in my assessment, I was struck by how much the video changed his Presence. Because his face was all we saw and it filled only the lower third of the video, he looked insignificant. Because the color of his jacket clashed with the background color in the room, his image was discordant.

And because the sound was not very good, his message was lost in his fast and somewhat inarticulate speech. Overall, the video environment diminished his Presence significantly — it worked against him.

Of course, connecting with others is not always easy even when we are with them in person. During the early days of my coaching business, I frequently spoke at business clubs like Rotary and networking groups for women. I used these opportunities to share my knowledge, test out my ideas, and refine my presentation skills. I often sang during those talks and one day I was invited to speak and sing at a dinner for a large group at a conference in a hotel. I jumped at the chance.

When I arrived that night, I saw that the "stage," located in a corner of a huge room, lacked adequate lighting and sound equipment, and looking out from the corner it became clear that the audience was more interested in

 **INSIGHT**

Think of it this way, if you want a clear, strong Presence, you need a clear, strong image. To increase your presence on video, make sure your image takes up most of the screen. To aim the camera to support Presence, divide the screen into three equal horizontal portions. Position your eyes at the bottom of the upper third. Also be sure you have a great mic that produces a clear, strong audio so your voice is strong and clear, too. What people experience of you is how they think of you.

networking than listening to me or anyone else. I felt a sense of dread and uncertainty creeping in, but despite the less-than-ideal setup, I gathered my composure and began my show. I quickly noticed that the general lighting failed to shift to stage lighting, and the microphone repeatedly produced a deafening squeal of feedback despite my efforts to control it.

As if things couldn't get worse, the audience began to engage in conversation, making it difficult for me to capture their attention. Undaunted, I forged ahead, doing everything I could to get them to listen. I walked among the crowd. I stared at people until they were embarrassed enough to momentarily stop talking with their companions. I got dramatic. But despite my efforts to adapt my delivery and draw the audience's focus, we never quite got there.

The experience was overwhelmingly frustrating and embarrassing, and I may have worked harder that night than ever before or since, but it taught me two things. First, the crucial lesson that connecting with people can be dependent on having all technical and environmental aspects properly arranged. Second, that getting people to listen is not about speaking or singing louder or embarrassing them. It's about relating as if you were sitting next to them at dinner where you can see each other's expressions and join in with each other's emotions.

Today, presenting on a video platform can feel like what I felt at that dinner. The sound could be better, and the lighting is difficult to adjust, even with a Ring camera. Getting the environment just right to keep people engaged is a challenge. A presenter can easily feel like the background to whatever everyone else is doing, such as emailing or chasing the dog. Helpfully, every virtual meeting platform publishes information on conducting meetings successfully, and most businesspeople have become experienced at the ins and outs of video calls on various platforms. Cameras are improving, and the good ones also have good microphones. Technology companies are racing to create mics that don't pick up the gardener or your dog. But it's the human connection that we still have to get right.

To participate successfully as presenters, we must plan to shine a light on our humanity. Technology will keep improving and it can help but it only works with what we give it. How we are framed in the camera and the sound are important factors to get right. Fortunately, we also have great personal assets that are even more important than cameras in a virtual world and they are what is often missing in virtual meetings. We have voices and faces that can be amazingly expressive. We can explore that and improve our Presence. Our capability to tell and appreciate stories is innate. We can find content that is Story rather than mere content. Mostly, if we prepare with the Intention to engage and choose to be present as one human to another, we can connect even when the technology and environment are against us.

TIPS AND TRICKS

Tips to maintain Presence during video conferences:

- First, set yourself up with the Intention to participate and be accountable for the call. Think about your Story and the purpose for the call ahead of time so you are prepared with something meaningful to say. Get away from distractions and plan to show up on video.
- As people gather, take that time to say a few words and inquire about what's going on in other people's lives. Those five minutes align well with the Intention to participate.
- Use a good camera and microphone for best sound quality and to optimize the video image so your Presence reflects your desire to participate. Test your equipment ahead of time so the lighting is complimentary, and you look present. Frame your face so that your eyes are positioned at the bottom of the top third of the picture. Avoid wearing clothing with stripes and intricate patterns.
- Chime in at least every 7-10 minutes so others feel and see your Presence. Participate if there is an interactive moment.
- Use expressive language when sharing ideas. i.e., I am delighted with the terrific results, or, conversely, we have a critical issue that requires our undivided attention. This may take some practice, but it will greatly add to Presence and increase your impact. As part of preparation, consider the topic and find something you can talk about that inspires or motivates you to chime into the discussion. Bring the passion in your Story to the call.

IS INTERRUPTING AN INTERRUPTION?

On video calls, we have learned to tolerate interruptions by children, pets, and package deliveries. Some of those interruptions are endearing because they break down the walls that separate the various parts of our lives. They connect our work lives to our home lives and may even remind us of our common humanity.

During the pandemic, I was grateful to be able to conduct coaching sessions through virtual meetings. One interesting aspect of working remotely is the unexpected interruptions that can occur even when we are striving to maintain a professional environment. I have encountered many such instances, but one of my favorites involves a client whose child excitedly entered the room during our session. The little girl joyfully exclaimed, "I got in!" before climbing onto her father's lap and hugging him tightly. Shortly after, I saw another figure enter the room, crouched down and walking like a crab in the sand, trying to avoid being seen on camera. It was the mom, and she whispered loudly, "No, no, no. Daddy's working! You have to stay in the other room!"

After peeling the girl off his neck, my client reassured her that he was working, and she needed to stay with her mom. As the little girl, still enthusiastic, was ushered out of the room, we heard her call out, "I want to work, too!" Following the interruption, my client apologized profusely, but I was not at all bothered. In fact, I found the situation endearing and gained a new appreciation for him and the challenges of working from home.

Another more insidious disturbance that often occurs in meetings, however, is the habit of interrupting others on the call. It has long been a problem in business meetings but has become a more significant issue with the increase in remote work. Bandwidth restrictions interfere with both audio and visual clarity. As soon as there are more than four people on a call, it's challenging to follow ordinary discourse, let alone one where we are unclear about who is speaking.

Then there's the problem of gender inequality in conversations. In their oft-cited study from 1975 "Sex Roles, Interruptions and Silences in Conversations," sociologists Don Zimmerman and Candace West shed light on the power dynamics in conversations between men and women. Analyzing 31 recordings of two-party conversations in public settings, they found that instances of interruption were significantly higher in mixed-gender conversations compared to same-sex interactions. The data revealed that men interrupted women 33% more often than they interrupted other men, highlighting a clear gender imbalance in conversational dynamics.

Although this issue still exists today, women are learning strategies to cope. We've also learned that interrupting is not simply a gender issue. Traditionally, we feel people interrupt each other to complete their turn or stop another person from completing theirs. However, research at Stanford shows that people view interruptions differently depending on whether they are high-intensity or low-intensity speakers.[55] In

---

55   Shashkevich, Alex. (2025 November 08). "Stanford Researcher Examines How People Perceive Interruptions in Conversation." *Stanford Report*. https://news.stanford.edu/2018/05/02/exploring-interruption-conversation/

the first category, everyone talking at the same time is a sign of engagement. People who view interruptions this way may also be uncomfortable with silence. On the other hand, low-intensity speakers prefer people to speak one at a time. So, we ask, "Is interrupting an interruption?" The answer is, to some it is and to some it is not.

No matter which way one views interruptions, it takes patience to have conversations. For some, the Intention to be heard trumps the fact that others want to be heard, too. This may mean that we cannot let go of our own position enough to hear others. We've talked about listening and inquiry already, and those are enormously useful, even essential in conversations and meetings. For those most likely to interrupt others, listening and inquiry are the key; we cannot know what others are willing to listen to if we don't also listen to them. On the other hand, no matter how good we are at listening, when it's time to respond or to share a point of view, sometimes it's hard to find the space for it. For those who are constantly interrupted, a little strategy is useful.

 **TIPS AND TRICKS**

How can you deal with interruptions effectively?

1.   **Speak up.** If your Intention is to be heard, keep focused on that Intention and align your Presence with it. You may need to speak louder or stronger. You may need to stand up to be heard. Even in virtual calls, standing up gives you more

energy and Presence. Keeping your Intention to be heard in mind, you'll find it easier to be confident, loud, and strong.

2. **Find someone to advocate for you**. There may be someone else in the room or on the call who sees you struggling or has struggled to be heard. Speak with them ahead of time to ask for support if you think you may run into difficulty dealing with interruptions. Conversely, if you don't have problems with interruptions but see others trying to be heard, advocate for them.

3. **Turnabout is fair play.** If you don't listen to others, why should they listen to you? Instead, set your Intention to hear and be heard and align your Story with that Intention. Make sure that when others speak you let them know you've heard them by paraphrasing their comments and ask them to confirm that what you thought you heard was indeed "IT!"

4. **Become comfortable with silence**. Let your Presence show that you value other's contributions and set your Intention to be inclusive. Take a breath rather than take a turn. Listen more and talk less. Of course, taking a pause when sharing your thoughts may signal to others that they can jump in even if you are not finished. So, if there is silence between your words, there are ways to make it clear to others that you have more to say. Tell them kindly to wait, and keep your body language alert as an indicator, or hold up your hand toward them as if to say "stop." But don't be a conversation hog, either. That's out of alignment with an Intention to hear and be heard.

5. **Pay attention to what has heart and meaning**. People have feelings. Express yours and encourage others to do the same. Just stating and recognizing feelings can make all the difference in Story and Presence so they align with Intention. When you have something to say but feel overlooked others may feel the same way. Those doing the trampling may be irritated or even insensitive, but they are

still human. It's worth a try to speak up about wanting to be heard, perhaps also reminding others of the Intention for the discussion.

REFLECTION
THE GIFT OF PRESENCE

We don't have to be trained stage performers, and we don't have to be one of the "lucky few" who were born with an innate ability to charm a room. By choosing to focus on our vocal image, our gestures, our posture, and shaping our environment to support us, we can make quick, easy adjustments that will significantly enhance our Presence, especially when those are aligned with our Intention and Story. It won't happen overnight, but we will start to effect a change with practice. Presence is a choice. It is also a gift.

Gifts are items we choose and give to others. When we select a gift, we typically consider the recipient so we can give them the most appropriate gift. Not everyone takes this first step, which underscores its importance. We notice when it is there, and we notice when it is not! Presence is a choice as well, and we notice when it is thoughtfully chosen

If we desire, we can change our Presence just as we would select a different present for different people. Don't you love getting a present that reminds you of the giver — a present that comes from the heart and seems chosen especially with you in mind? Similarly, choosing to connect with others at a human level, to be true to your heart, values, and beliefs creates the best Presence of all – your authentic Presence.

When it comes to giving, we can share our Presence by simply sitting and listening while others talk or stand up in front and make our Presence felt. We can look others in the eye and acknowledge their Presence, too. But the most beautiful part of Presence is how it gives back — when we share our authentic Presence, others feel more comfortable sharing theirs. In that way, if we are genuinely present, Presence is a present.

CHAPTER 4

THE FINAL PRINCIPLE, **REVERBERATION**

"Good conversation has an edge: it opens your eyes to something, quickens your ears. And good conversation reverberates: it keeps on talking in your mind later in the day."

– James Hillman

 **WHAT YOU WILL LEARN**

CHAPTER 4: REVERBERATION

When your message echoes in minds and lives.

What You'll Learn
- How Intention, Story, and Presence combine to create lasting impact.
- What "Reverberation" means in communication — not just sound.
- How to use Reverberation principles in meetings, conversations, and conflicts.
- How to spot (and fix) blocks to being heard — like vocal fatigue or fear.
- Real-world strategies to be more impactful and inspiring.

Key Takeaways
- Your voice is heard when your message aligns deeply and lands fully, no matter the occasion.
- To Reverberate is to communicate not as a performance, but as relationship.
- To Reverberate is to create connection, trust, and shared movement—without sacrificing who you are.

UNDERSTANDING REVERBERATION

Earlier we defined Reverberation in context of auditory harmonics: "When sound strikes a surface, it's reflected at varying times and amplitudes, creating an echo which conveys complex information about the sound, the physical space through which it travelled, and the source from which it emanated." We then likened Reverberation to the alignment of Intention, Story, and Presence. Simply put, "The better aligned these are — the better they reverberate with each other and align with the audience — the more significant the impact."

Looking more closely at the phenomenon of reverberation we see it is made up of harmonics. Harmonics comprise multiple integers of the base frequency recurring at regular intervals. This internal consistency is why harmonics are so... well, harmonious.

People have played with reverberation for centuries. Today, reverberation effects, or "reverb," are used in sound studios to enhance depth, but the Tuvan throat singers as far back as 220 BC have experimented with vocal overtones and used their reverberation to commune with nature and heighten spiritual experiences.

A friend of mine who is a professional singer was interested in overtone chanting and introduced me to the album *Hearing Solar Winds,* performed by The Harmonic Choir, led by David Hykes. You can hear vocal overtones at play in this fascinating record.

The album was recorded by Radio France on the nights of

August 6 and 7 in 1982 at l'Abbaye du Thoronet, a 12th-century Cistercian monastery in Provence. The seven performers construct nine pieces of music based on the natural overtones of the human voice. To bring out the overtones so we can hear them, they greatly elongate vowel sounds, controlling the harmonics by mouth shape, tongue position, volume, and breath control. The result is a rich feast for the ear – long, low notes with flute-like sounds dancing far above the base tones. The music also has a beautifully calming effect on my body, inducing a sense of tranquility and peace.

When I heard it, I was captivated by the sound and tried it myself in several resonant places at home. It was fun and almost hypnotic, so I admit to being a bit jealous that they were doing this in such a wonderful environment and, I assume, being paid for it!

Apart from the incredible performance, what is also remarkable about the recording of *Hearing Solar Winds* is the reverberation. Reverberation doesn't just happen the moment the sound is produced. It persists even after the source of sound has stopped. We can hear it in the echoing ring of the voices of the Harmonic Choir, after they stop singing. This happens due to the reflection of the sound waves on the hard surfaces of the monastery chapel, and for us more modern humans, surfaces such as furniture, people, and even air. The sound hits those surfaces and bounces back to be heard again.

Reverberation does wonders when it comes to musical

symphonies and orchestra halls, or overtone chanting in monasteries. When the right amount of reverberation is present, the sound quality gets enhanced drastically. It's why everyone sounds better singing in the shower.

In the context of speaking with others, of having impact with that communication, Reverberation also creates a lasting impression of the speaker and their ideas. When we achieve Reverberation, our metaphorical voice has depth and quality that resounds in the minds and hearts of listeners. It has an impact that is memorable, enhancing the message much as a sound wave is enriched in an auditorium. Just as the reverberation in a concert hall can be controlled to augment the sound, so can the impact we have as speakers be controlled and strengthened by aligning our Intention, Story, and Presence.

Reverberation has a downside, too. This mostly occurs within a confined area. As sound continues to reflect and reverberate, noise builds up. Reverberation in a room impacts speech intelligibility and the quality of sound due to the muffled and repeatedly bounced-around sound waves. We've probably all experienced this effect if we've been to a sporting event in a gymnasium. Often, the liveliness of the reverberation is so great that it is hard to understand the announcer.

The same thing can happen when we communicate. If we are out of balance, our ideas get muddled and so do our words. We may have great Intention, but if it isn't reflected in our words it can lead to a weak and confusing Presence. We might know what we want to say but not why we want to say it, or how. Perhaps we already have a clear Intention and a great Story, but we're terrified to put ourselves out there, or we don't quite have the vocal skills we need to convey our ideas. Just as noise builds up with uncontrolled reverberation, these misalignments will leave a muddled rather than memorable impression on listeners and conversation partners.

Throughout the book, we have explored some of the deeper intricacies of Intention, Story, and Presence. During that process, we discovered areas where these forces intersect, and we learned the importance of linking and intertwining them in our communications. We will now take a closer look at some ways to work with Intention, Story, and Presence so that we can achieve Reverberation and have a lasting positive impact on our audiences, whether it be a board presentation, a town hall event, or a personal conversation.

AUTHENTICITY FUELS REVERBERATION

When I first started working with business professionals, I believed my background as a performer would be an asset. After all, who wouldn't want to be on stage? However, my perspective changed one day when I was introduced to a potential client, Jess. Jess had been referred to me by someone who appreciated our work together, and we arranged a "chemistry" call to see if we could collaborate. Since she was in a different time zone, our call took place relatively late on a weekday, and I was tired after a long day.

We exchanged pleasantries and discussed her needs. Jess mentioned that she was looking for help in communicating more effectively with her executive team, which was crucial for her as she was hoping for a promotion. The conversation flowed comfortably, and we even chatted about books we had read and movies we had seen recently. I felt confident that we would be a great match.

Then she asked how I got into my work, and I shared my experience in performing and the years spent as a professional musician. Suddenly, her tone shifted, and she said she needed to leave but would be in touch. I assumed something urgent had come up. Two weeks later, I received a message from her. She expressed her interest in working with me but admitted she had almost changed her mind when I mentioned my performing career. She said, "I am not an actor, and I don't want to be one."

Jess was the first one to say that, but not the last. Some businesspeople are suspicious of my background as a performer, and there are others who believe that showing up as authentic should be effortless. Over time, I've become more comfortable in talking about the link between my background and what businesspeople can get from someone like me. The truth is, while there may be some overlap between communication skills and acting, learning to be a better communicator is primarily focused on developing practical skills for effective, genuine communication in a variety of contexts. Acting, on the other hand, is focused on the performance of a specific, usually fictional role or character.

Although I see that we all play different roles in our lives, I am focused on paring away "acting" and getting to "authentic." Finding our unique voice is not about copying someone else's voice or pretending to be someone we are not.

What then constitutes authenticity in communication? Harvard professor Amy Cuddy is quoted as saying, "Authenticity doesn't just mean you're not filtering what you're saying, it's about being able to know and access the best parts of yourself and bring them forward."[56] Isn't this what we all want to see in each other — people who are committed to values, driven by solid beliefs in a vision and comfortable in their own skin? Authenticity is a natural outcome when all parts of our communication are aligned — when we have Reverberation — so rather than appearing as an actor playing a part, we appear as trustworthy being ourselves.

For most of us, it takes years. As Carl Jung said, "The privilege of a lifetime is to become who you truly are." In the business world of today, one cannot afford to show up as untrustworthy or inauthentic no matter how legitimate the personal quest. Most people don't strive to show up that way, rather they show up as inauthentic because they're afraid to show their true selves, fearing they may not be accepted, or believing that they need to have a prescribed persona to be successful. Sometimes, inauthenticity is a result of an ingrained habit or mannerism we picked up

---

56   Cuddy, Amy. *Presence: Bringing Your Boldest Self to Your Biggest Challenges.* Little, Brown & Company, 2016.

somewhere earlier in life.

Not long ago, a vibrant female business woman, whom we'll refer to as Joann, came to me with a concern that weighed heavily on her. At the end of long, demanding days at the office, she often found herself leaving work with a raspy voice and an overwhelming sense of exhaustion. All she longed for was a quiet evening at home, wrapped in a cozy blanket, lost in the pages of a good book, desperately trying to tune out the chaos of the day.

Joann admitted that her job had become particularly stressful. She was laser-focused on securing much-needed funding for her rapidly expanding company, yet the frequent strain on her voice was a baffling and troubling new issue she had to confront. We dedicated time to rehabilitating her voice, helping her raise her pitch and cultivating resonance to reduce the strain she was experiencing. To her surprise, lifting the burdensome weight from her voice was not as difficult as she expected. Still, it took time for her to adjust and feel comfortable speaking in this new manner because it felt unnatural at first.

Joann has a naturally gregarious spirit. She has a gift for storytelling, infusing each narrative with rich detail and vibrant imagery that makes any topic come alive. Her communication style is mostly clear, compelling, and strong. She wields humor skillfully, effortlessly drawing others into conversation — all elements of an exceptional communicator. This still came through after she adopted a healthier vocal style. She was still Joann. I couldn't shake the feeling, however, that one particular vocal characteristic was inadvertently standing in the way of her fundraising aspirations.

Taking a leap of faith, I inquired about her experiences with securing funding, specifically regarding her presentations to potential investors. Joann confessed that although she didn't frighten her audience, she was also struggling to close deals. I suggested that she present her pitch to me. As I suspected, her content was indeed clear and engaging, but the cadence of her voice – the rhythm and flow – was misaligned with her Story and Intention.

The aspect that made Joann's speaking style endearing was her habitual use of that upward pitch or open cadence at the end of her sentences, which added engagement and warmth into her conversations. Unfortunately, she applied this friendly cadence even when making declarative statements. This tendency often led to her coming across as indecisive and, at worst, wishy-washy – a perception that could be detrimental when trying to persuade potential investors.

Eager to refine her approach and secure the support her company needed, Joann was open to experimenting with her vocal style. We focused on adjusting her cadence and enhancing various elements of her vocal delivery. Remarkably, she began to observe a transformation in her communication. Before long, she not only secured the investments she sought but also left work each day feeling accomplished and fulfilled rather than drained.

Today, Joann is recognized as both authoritative and approachable. She has honed her ability to make intentional vocal choices, effectively balancing the need to close a critical deal or make a casual connection, adapting her vocal strategies to suit each unique scenario while still showing up as genuine, which she is.

Authenticity is an important topic of this century. Perhaps it's because of the introduction of CGI with films and the ever-expanding world of AI, perhaps it is the proliferation of fake news in social media, perhaps it is just human nature. Whatever the reason, it seems we question what is real more than ever. Sadly, we know that fakes abound. Phishing scams, cyberattacks, and identity theft constitute a booming industry founded upon imposters posing as something they're not. We are swimming in an ocean of inauthenticity.

The search to find one's authentic voice in today's environment can feel like a true existential crisis. When it comes to an individual and personal basis, what does it mean to be authentic? If we are self-aware and willing to learn more about who we are, does that make us authentic? Would we even know our authentic self if we found it?

The secret is to be as authentic as we can be in the moment. Intention-driven communication allows us to do that. Intention is the aim that guides action. When we get clear about why we are saying and doing what we are saying and doing, we have a greater chance of being authentic. We can then consider our choice of words accordingly, and we can deliver them with confidence and candor so that all parts of our communication Reverberate without contradiction.

To do this, it is critical to ask deep questions and use the answers to shape communication. Authenticity takes time and deliberation. So does Reverberation. When preparing a presentation, most businesspeople spend more time on Story than anything else. In fact, many people tell me their Intention is so simple it doesn't need to be documented. Although Story is important, starting with a good exploration of our Intention and giving equal time to Presence will ensure better alignment of the three.

 **TIPS AND TRICKS**

Here is an easy-to-use self-inventory for aligning Intention, Story, and Presence. Taking time to answer each of these questions and document your responses will help to reveal areas of misalignment and more, importantly, areas to strengthen to ensure Reverberation.

1. Who is my audience and what do they care about? What is their frame of mind right now? What emotional filters are they using?

2. What do I want to accomplish and how am I going to get there?

3. What is my call to action? What do I want others to do because of having this conversation/hearing this presentation?

4. Do I have a hidden agenda? For example, if you say you simply want to give some information, are you in fact looking to persuade someone to your point of view? Be honest with yourself. (see page 215 about conversational intention)

5. What words, stories, format will I use in support of

my Intention? What is the right tone of voice for this communication? What is my empowerment promise (page 85)? How will I surprise them? What kind of Story will be best?

6. How do I want to show up? What is the best environment for this communication? Will I sit or stand? Will it be in person or virtual? What is my emotional state regarding this communication? What will I wear? What time of day will it be and how do I feel about that?

7. How does my body feel about this communication? Excited? Nervous? Happy? Sad? Angry? Blasé? Confident? Insecure? Ready? Not ready? What can I do to prepare to show up as my best self?

 **INSIGHT**

When thinking through your observations, you might want to write them down. One way to do that is to create a mind map. Although you can find software online for mind mapping, it's very easy to do with a piece of paper and some colored pencils. You could use pens, of course, but I learned early that a good musician always carries a pencil since you never know when the conductor or director will change their mind about the instructions they gave in the previous rehearsal. Mind mapping should be similarly unrestricted by permanence.

How to Mind Map

- Start with a blank page.
- Use an image or word for your central idea and place it in the middle of the page.
- Draw main branches that connect to the central image.
- Use one key word or image per branch using different colors to indicate different ideas.
- In a similar manner, create smaller branches that connect to the main branches as needed until you have captured all of your ideas.

STATEMENT OF INTENT AND REVERBERATION

If you want to be seen as inspiring, you have to inspire, which is where a Statement of Intention comes in. We discussed its value in the chapter on Story. As a reminder, it is an affirmational statement we use to shape how we, as presenters, speakers and even writers, show up. Its success lies in the use of mental plasticity to begin to shape how we see ourselves. If you haven't created one, go back to page 56 and complete the exercise. Craft it carefully and thoughtfully because it is the headlamp that will illuminate the path to the optimal impact.

By taking stock of our strengths and what's most important to us about our role or aspirational role, we figure out how we want others to perceive us, and it is usually our best, authentic selves that we describe. Some people have likened it to a personal brand statement, which is not far off. The difference is that its purpose is not self-marketing but self-devolvement – greater Presence and more powerful communication of Story that connects through the alignment with clear Intention.

An SOI (Statement of Intention) serves as a powerful visualization tool. I discovered the impact of visualizations in my 20s through the inspiring writings of Viktor Frankl, the esteemed psychiatrist. Frankl faced horrific challenges and personal losses while interned in Auschwitz, yet he emerged stronger by envisioning himself delivering lectures to his students after liberation. This remarkable ability to visualize his future as a professor in American colleges allowed him to transcend his dire circumstances and assert his freedom as a human being.

Athletes exemplify the effectiveness of visualization in achieving extraordinary feats. Many elite competitors, including Michael Phelps (swimming), Lindsey Vonn (skiing), LeBron James (basketball), Ronaldinho (soccer), Katie Ledecky (swimming), Richard Sherman (football), and Serena Williams (tennis), harness mental imagery and affirmations to maximize their performance. By regularly employing these techniques, they push the limits of their abilities and heighten their chances of success in the most intense competitions. Their triumphs may be seen as Reverberation at its best as they align their purpose and goals with a plan to get there, the skills, knowledge, and behaviors needed, and the application in competitions.

When we create a personal SOI, the process asks us to inventory qualities that resonate with us, behaviors that we appreciate and want to see more of. The verbs and descriptors we use can shape our behavior as well as our Story. But SOI's are not magical. Having one does not guarantee metamorphosis. What is necessary is to put them to work by regularly reviewing them and letting them intentionally guide us to become the person we describe. In other words:

- If I want to be seen as inspirational, I must inspire.
- If I want to be seen as collaborative, I must talk about

someone besides myself.

- If I want to be seen as innovative, I can help others use their imaginations.

REVERBERATION IN PRACTICE

It has been over 2400 years since Aristotle expounded on theoria (thinking), poiesis (making), and praxis (doing). Regardless of the passage of years with all its technological advancements, these are still essential concepts. With that in mind, we have spent a fair amount of time establishing the theory of Reverberation. Now let's explore more about the *making* so that we can be more comfortable and confident in the *doing*.

At the request of a leader in the insurance industry, I attended a two-hour "all-hands" meeting. Having participated in many large meetings like this, I've often been surprised to see top businesspeople who seem uncomfortable and unprepared for such critical events. In this instance, I was aware that the staff had been preparing for weeks. They were proud to start with an expensive introductory video. The organization placed a high value on communication plans, and the in-house communications team spent many late nights refining the presenters' scripts to perfection. The room was adorned with motivational banners. Every seat was filled and there were an additional 800 people logging in online.

Despite all the preparation, most of the presenters went over their allotted time and tended to look at the screen behind them or at the floor rather than engaging with the audience. Their presentations were monotonous recitations of facts and figures, accompanied by slides that contained too much text. People in the room were squirming in their chairs, struggling to stay awake. Even though the quarter's performance had been good, the numbers themselves failed to engage people. The sterile atmosphere of the room, with its corporate multi-purpose design, and the uninteresting lighting did not help. Fortunately, there were cookies available at the end of the meeting; everyone would need a bit of sugar to keep from heading back to their cubicles for a nap!

Then, a presenter stepped up to discuss the quarterly results. Suddenly, the audience was captivated. What made the difference was the speaker, particularly their use of what Toastmasters International refers to as "vocal variety."

As Bill Brown says in *Toastmaster Magazine*, "Vocal variety is more than merely avoiding the dreaded monotone. It is, at its foundation, the life that you breathe into what you say and do onstage."[57]

The truth of this principle lies in the fact that even though people have learned to generate voices with AI that sound very human-like, the last frontier is expression. The degree to which we use expression is the physical manifestation of how much we have or have not aligned Intention, Presence, and Story. In short, how well we Reverberate.

---

57   Brown, Bill. (2025 November 08). "Why Vocal Variety Is So Valuable." *Toastmasters International*.   https://www.toastmasters.org/magazine/magazine-issues/2020/sept/ toolbox-why-vocal-variety-is-so-valuable

Later an audience member wrote an email to her boss saying: *"I don't know if it's P.C. to tell your VP that he was rocking today on the broadcast, although today was one of those days! I held my team call after the IPTV, and EVERYONE was extremely impressed."*

Evocative words and vocal variety are Story tools that serve to expose multi-layered meaning in our communication. As we learned in the chapter on Presence, vocal variety, or what I call inflection, is a part of Presence that is particularly important in the English language, which requires nuance and pauses to create meaning out of words.

In theater, actors practice saying the same line with different inflections to change the meaning. By placing more vocal emphasis, or stress, on some words, the sense of the sentence changes. Try this simple sentence as an example:

"**I** don't think you will like the movie."

"I **don't** think you will like the movie."

"I don't **think** you will like the movie."

"I don't think **you** will like the movie."

"I don't think you will **like** the movie."

"I don't think you will like **the movie**."

Notice how simply changing the inflection changes how the statement is cast as well as received. You can also turn statements into questions and vice versa with inflection. By shifting tone and volume, you can fill words and sentences with humor, anger, joy, and sadness.

Several years ago, I held a workshop for business people

working for an American company in Bengaluru, India. The participants were mostly locals with English as their second or even third or fourth language. Most had been asked at one time or another by their native-English-speaking colleagues to slow down so they could be understood. Keeping in mind that these were global business people, it was especially important that they could be understood.

First, we did an exercise to determine the pace of their speech. We discovered most were flying along between 200 - 220 words per minute (wpm). For context, English is best understood between 140-180 wpm. Making things more difficult was the fact that fast languages such as Italian and Tamil (Southern India) create meaning by using more syllables per minute — e.g., saying more words. Although many people in southern India speak English, most of them learned it from someone whose native language was also a Southern Indian language, which means the characteristics were simply shifted to their English. As a result, they naturally became fast English speakers.

But the pace of their speaking was only part of the problem. Non-native talkers may not vary their intonations as much when they speak English as the language requires for comprehension. This deprives listeners of a valuable tool in understanding what the speaker is saying. Inflection in English is a spark that surprises and absorbs us in each other's communication. Without it, the language is flat and much less interesting. But, even with native English speakers, inflection doesn't come naturally to everyone or in every situation. In fact, notice that Bill Brown says we must do something to create vocal variety — specifically, breathe life into what we say and do. How does one do that?

Vocal variety is created by connecting conscious meaning (Intention) to words that light up the brains of our audience (Story) so that we emphasize those words to build tension or create impact (Presence). In this case, the tools we use to create that impact are aspects of sound; sound is a characteristic of Presence, the choice to show up a certain way.

Conversely, when we strive to create more vocal variety, we naturally become more aware of the *why* and *what* of our communication and their effect on *how* we say *what* we say. This ability to convey meaning in sound is available to almost all of us. For some it may take more work to become aware.

The ability to connect also requires a willingness to bring emotion into the spotlight. I had the unexpected opportunity to play with this idea in a workshop I held with college students at California State University, Fullerton. We had just been through the part of the workshop in which participants created their SOIs. I asked if someone would be willing to read theirs aloud to the group. Enthusiastically, a young woman volunteered. She had been a full participant in the workshop to that point, a self-proclaimed high achiever who was eager to take the world on at graduation. Her SOI was passionate and inspiring, containing a powerful vision for her future. However, she read it in a flat, expressionless tone almost as if she were embarrassed by what she was saying. I asked her to look at it closely and read it again with the same fervor as the words described and to see it as her purpose with a plan to get there.

After a couple of minutes studying the words, she read it again. This time cheers erupted from her classmates. The difference between the two readings was palpable. Just because I couldn't resist, I asked her to read it again but this time to insert "um" or "uh" and "kind of" every three words or so. Once again, everyone got the message. The filler words seriously detracted from the power of the beautiful statement even though the words in her SOI were the same as before. The lesson was that the alignment of Intention, Story, and Presence makes a noticeable difference.

 **TIPS AND TRICKS**

Here are eight ways to use vocal variety to connect and Reverberate:

1. **Vary the pace:** Keep your overall pace between 140-160 words per minute so that people can follow you. Speed up or slow down to build or ease tension.
2. **Vary the cadence:** Ending sentences always open or closed is boring. Make definitive statements but also ask open-ended questions and invite a response.
3. **Vary the pitch:** Varying pitch throughout creates interest in the ear of the listener. If you have a low voice, raise it in pitch from time to time for emphasis. If your voice is high, bring it down, especially when you make a definitive statement.
4. **Vary the duration of the sound:** Some words create a

mental picture that is slow (like that one) or quick (like that.) Let your voice paint that picture by drawing out the slo-o-o-w pictures and clipping words that describe something fast. To practice this, read something descriptive aloud and look for the words that are the most expressive. They are usually adjectives or adverbs. Stress the vowels in those words to help you craft a mental image of what they describe.

5. **Highlight contrasting ideas:** Not all ideas are the same. Consider this quote:

   - "The world is divided into those who eat chocolate without bread; those who cannot eat chocolate unless they also eat bread; those who don't have chocolate; those who do not have bread." - Stefano Benni, Italian novelist.

   - How can you use your voice to underscore the contrasting ideas? Here's one way: "The world is divided into those **who eat chocolate withOUT bread**; those who **cannot** eat chocolate **unless they ALso eat bread;** those who **don't** have **chocolate**; those who **do not** have **bread**."

6. **Stress words that add meaning:** Although in the above quote, context adds meaning to the repeated words bread and chocolate, the importance of the descriptors "without" and "also" is significant. My suggestion to stress them is indicated by capital letters and by stressing them we are more likely to convey the connotation of the quote.

7. **Create some mystery:** With the intention of capturing the audience's curiosity, a hushed tone creates a sense of mystery. When coupled with intriguing questions and provocative statements, the Reverberation is captivating.

8. **Let there be silence:** Don't keep talking without pausing. If you listen to singers, notice that it's rare for a singer to sing for the entire song. The other musicians may keep

playing, but there are usually times when the singer is not singing. You may also have noticed that an unexpected or extra-long moment of silence in a play or speech catches the audience's attention. When it comes to Reverberation, silence really is golden.

REVITALIZING MEETINGS

In the chapter on Intention, we learned how Intention can be used to shape or guide a meeting. Wouldn't it be great if all meetings were dynamic, collaborative, and productive? The good news is that we can shape meetings to Reverberate from the beginning and give everyone attending a chance to Reverberate as well.

Getting to that state comes more naturally than one might expect, especially with some practice. It is also received more readily than one might expect. For example, the desired Intention of a meeting might be: "We're going to take some time today to sketch out an outline of our project plan." This simple, open Statement of Intention gives people a clear idea of the purpose for the meeting and the plan to get there. However, what most people want is the space to interact with that Intention. Therefore, following the Intention statement with the question, "Are we agreed on this goal?" is a small gesture of seeking concurrence. It demonstrates a willingness to relinquish control and allow others to be partners in the path of the discussion. This check in establishes a baseline.

At this point there's likely to be some discussion about the purpose of the meeting. In fact, this is the very next step.

By taking time to invite others to share their own Intentions and listen to each other, people can agree on an Intention that works for everyone. Written down for everyone to see, the agreed goal may not be the exact one originally envisioned, but it will be a shared vision which all the parties can work towards. This makes the likelihood of success much higher because it is underpinned by trust. When we share something with another person, and when that person reciprocates by sharing in return, a bond of trust is formed.

As the meeting progresses, it's valuable to take periodic 'seismic readings.' That is, remind everyone of the baseline Intention and check to see if the meeting is staying focused. These readings prevent the conversation from getting stuck on details that can be handled in a different forum or tangents that have no bearing on the goal at hand.

It's still possible for a meeting to get off track, particularly if people are drawn into the weeds by a passionate puller. If the Intention is significantly shifting, it's imperative to call it out (or, as some people more aptly say, 'call it in'). Since everyone has agreed on the Intention, anyone in the meeting can say something like, "I think our Intention may be shifting somewhat. Let's talk about this and see if we need to make an adjustment."

To either identify a new Intention together or to reaffirm the original one, the most important thing is to be open with the discussion, which goes back to the importance of listening.

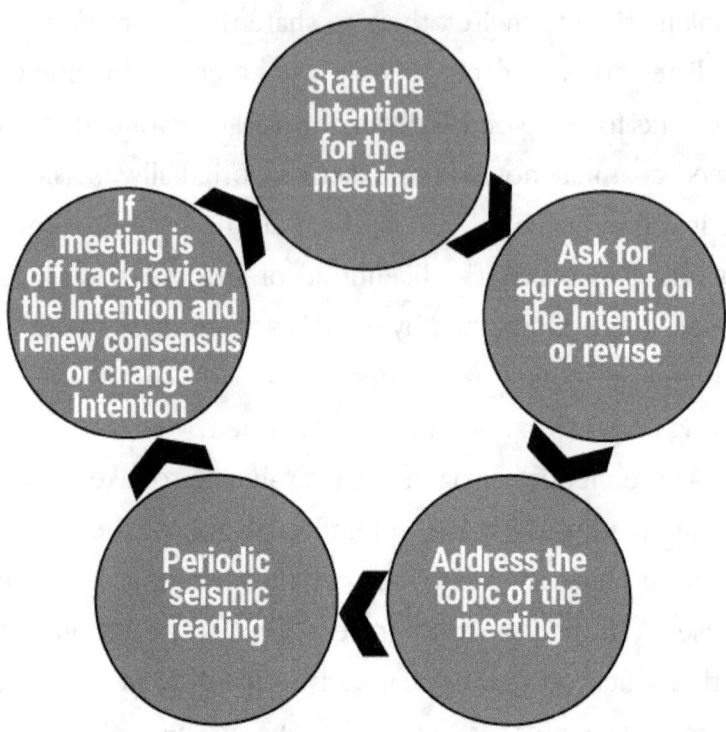

Of course, there are some challenges specific to virtual meetings. Turning on your camera used to be an option that few chose on conference calls, but with the use of virtual meetings becoming more prevalent, turning on the camera is more of a norm. Keep in mind, however, that this differs by region. In many Middle Eastern countries, for instance, not using the camera is the default mode. For those who do use cameras during video calls, it's important to learn about lighting, backgrounds, and microphones if we want to show up with Presence, which brings up another challenge, technology itself.

My personal experience with setting up a studio for online videos and podcasting was both promising and frustrating. I got help from my daughter who works in the music industry and her recording engineer partner and was excited to put my "easy-to-use" studio together. They helped me select equipment and expected I would be able to figure out how to make it all work. Simple for them; not so simple for me. The equipment remained in boxes until I had time to study and set it up. Even so it took a lot of trial and error to get it the way I wanted it. I've heard similar stories from people who buy a studio-in-a-box from an electronics store. Just because technology is getting easier to use doesn't mean it is simple for everyone.

Finally, the biggest difference between virtual and in-person communication is that even the best video and audio quality will minimize or obscure emotional cues, the cues we need to confirm comprehension and degrees of consensus. It's especially tricky to get the signals we need when all we see of our meeting companions is the top of their head and their ceiling fan spinning around above them.

Still, when approached with connection in mind even a virtual meeting can Reverberate. Elisha, the vice president leading a marketing division at a large semiconductor company, was gearing up for an important meeting with a group of analysts from a partner company. In preparation, we meticulously crafted a strategy, pinpointing the top three talking points in each area of interest while anticipating the questions and topics likely to arise during the discussion. I recognized that the key to a successful meeting lay not in diving straight into the technical details but in establishing a human connection first.

Knowing that Elisha had no prior acquaintance with the analysts, we brainstormed ways to break the ice and forge a bond. He could observe their surroundings and comment on the unique elements of their environment. Perhaps he could initiate the meeting with light-hearted small talk about a current sporting event, an intriguing world occurrence, or even the unpredictable weather — anything to encourage them to engage and open up. Why take this approach? Because nurturing a connection fosters an atmosphere of trust and ultimately leads to greater impact. While Elisha was initially skeptical about this strategy's effectiveness, he decided to give it a try.

The results astonished him. First, the analysts welcomed the opportunity for casual conversation and the meeting began in a more relaxed tone than Elisha had anticipated. But more surprising was what happened to create the most memorable moment of the meeting. While he was in the midst of delivering a report, a loud crash erupted in the background — the unmistakable sound of his wife dropping a large pan in the kitchen. The noise was so jarring that it could not be ignored. After ensuring that his wife was okay, Elisha quickly explained that it was Passover and she was cooking for a significant family gathering. He politely requested their understanding regarding the commotion.

In a delightful twist, one of the analysts chimed in with a question: "Is she making brisket?" This simple inquiry revealed that he, too, shared Elisha's Jewish background. With that, the atmosphere shifted dramatically, as the conversation effortlessly flowed into anecdotes about cherished Seder foods and family traditions. They exchanged stories about the custom of leaving the door open for Elijah and one shared a humorous tale of a mischievous neighborhood cat who had taken advantage of that invitation to sneak in and devour leftover chicken bones.

Elisha left the meeting with a warm feeling of connection — an unexpected bond formed through shared experiences. He carried with him not only confidence that the rest of the conversation had gone exceptionally well but also the realization that the initial rapport they built played a crucial role in the meeting's success.

Meetings will always be fraught with the potential to go wrong. Many people see meetings as a waste of time, drawing them away from their real work; some prefer face-to-face meetings while others prefer virtual.

As we learn more about how to use technology, let's remember that it is merely a tool that enables us to connect. In fact, meetings are tools to enable us to connect better and the best way to make that connection meaningful for everyone involved is through Reverberation. Reverberation is not about getting everything right when we are in front of an audience or in a conversation; Reverberation is about aligning all parts of our communication to create authentic connection that is memorable and inspires action.

TIPS AND TRICKS

How to create a meeting that Reverberates

- **Preparation:** Thinking ahead will help set the stage for a better meeting experience for everyone. For the owner of the meeting, planning is an essential part of the alignment that creates Reverberation. Consider who will be there (Presence), plan to involve them all and create a structure (Story) to accomplish the Intention of the meeting. Participants can also plan by thinking through ideas and preparing to bring them to the group.

- **Intention:** A good meeting has a clear purpose and a plan to get there. We are all too busy to waste our time convening just to have a meeting. A clear Intention helps the planning as well as the progress of a meeting and is best when it is made known to all ahead of time. Intention is also a terrific tool to keep participants from wandering off track in discussions. To set the Intention for a meeting, we can ask, "What do we plan to accomplish and how do we want to get there?" The answer is the Intention that informs both the Story and Presence for the meeting. It will also inform the call to action.

- **Connection:** Meetings are always better when people feel connected. Business is about people not just processes. Taking time to share common experiences (Story) brings people closer together. In-person meetings are enhanced with time to introduce or catch up with each other (Presence). Many people report that they relax more once they recognize others as people rather than titles or roles. We can see the proof of this when we consider how we share our home spaces in virtual meetings and enjoy noticing each other's environments, commenting on them, and learning about each other. Making time for stories brings a new level of interest to any meeting. Story is such an essential part of connection that training is well worthwhile.

- **Inquiry:** A good meeting has the spirit of people wanting to learn from each other along with creativity leading to unexpected solutions (Presence). In most meetings, encouraging questions rather than answers (Story) is more productive than coming in with a set of solutions. Inquiry encourages listening and creates an environment of openness (Presence), one where everyone has a voice, not just the few. This approach opens the door to a deeper kind of thinking, one that enables unexpected solutions, and it's well worth exploring.

- **Opportunity to have an impact:** Good meetings create meaningful output (Intention). They inspire people through significant content (Story) and the energy with which it is presented (Presence)to do something necessary or desirable. Attendees feel charged up to finish the report, learn more about the situation, and find a better solution or otherwise meet the call to action, thereby fulfilling the Intention.

REDISCOVERING CONVERSATIONS

Most people have anxiety about meeting new people. In a new job, performance anxiety is pressing, just as it is when attending a conference or a networking event. Cocktail parties can be sheer terror, especially when everyone there is a stranger. Most of the anxiety comes from fear of what to say in those first conversations.

I used to think there was a time-tested solution, the Dale Carnegie method. Carnegie recommended that to minimize the nerves about meeting people and reduce anxiety, one should ask questions and let others do the talking. The approach stems from Carnegie's theory that the best way to become interesting to others is to be interested in them. What I have discovered, however, is that while listening to others doesn't necessarily get me any more dinner invitations, it does minimize my exposure during interactions.

Even though focusing on others may help us get familiar enough with them to find common ground and relieve our anxiety, the solution to discomfort in social settings is not to pepper people with questions. Instead, ask yourself this: What if they feel just as uncomfortable conversing with a stranger as I do? After all, I don't know them, and they don't know me, so if they do all the talking, I may feel better, but I am still a stranger to them. New research confirms that "after engaging in 12-minute interactions (with strangers), listeners liked speakers more than speakers liked listeners because listeners felt more similar to speakers than speakers did to listeners."[58]

In a lead up to a MasterClass on storytelling, humorist and writer David Sedaris declares the right type of questions can yield wonderful stories from others. On the type of

---

58 Hirschi, Quinn. "People Think They Should Talk Less to Be Liked, But New Research Suggests You Should Speak Up in Conversations with Strangers." *The Conversation.* https://theconversation.com/people-think-they-should-talk-less-to-be-liked-but-new-research-suggests-you-should-speak-up-in-conversations-with-strangers-188196

questions, Sedaris says: "If it's a question you've heard in a hotel or a store, forget it."[59] He talks about a time when he asked a driver, "Have you ever run for office?" The surprised driver responded to a delighted Sedaris, "I can't believe you asked me that. I ran for judge 20 years ago in my town."

The point in all of this is you don't have to be David Sedaris to initiate great conversations, but you do have to step out there. As he aptly put it: "You need to be in the world, and you need to be engaged with the world."

I remember a train journey from Spain to France, where I had the opportunity to share a compartment with ten students and a nun. Our group was wonderfully diverse, with students from Spain, France, England, Italy, and Austria — while I represented the U.S. The nun, a remarkable individual from Spain, spoke Spanish, French, German, and Italian, but no English. I spoke a little of each language but was not fluent in any but English. My limited vocabulary in each language meant that I caught fragments of conversations but could not really communicate with anyone, or so I thought.

At first, our compartment was filled with hushed murmurs as we focused on conversing within our country groups or watching the world go by. With my limited knowledge of the other languages, I was busy eavesdropping to see what I could pick up. Then the nun broke the ice by individually asking about us and our travels. Soon after, she began introducing

---

59 Sedaris, David. (2025 November 08). "Observing the World." *MasterClass*. https://www.masterclass.com/classes/david-sedaris-teaches-storytelling-and-humor/chapters/observing-the-world

us to each other. Through her engaging introductions in multiple languages, she created an atmosphere of curiosity and openness. With her as the facilitator, she encouraged us to speak, to use our foreign language skills however haltingly, and to truly listen and learn from each other's experiences.

What became clear during our conversation was that understanding goes beyond language; it requires a willingness to connect and to be curious about different perspectives. As we exchanged stories and insights, I realized that this shared learning experience made our interactions meaningful.

The mistake many people make is convincing themselves that others are better communicators than they are. I clearly felt that way about the nun in my story, and it never occurred to me that she may not have been at all comfortable meeting strangers either; I've learned that most people, even those who appear perfectly confident may feel self-conscious about meeting new people.

In 2022 a group of researchers published a study that found that most people consistently underestimate how much they will enjoy speaking with strangers and how satisfied they will feel when they have meaningful conversations with anyone, including people they don't know.[60] Taking a chance by having deeper conversations with strangers can lead to more ease in unfamiliar social settings and, who knows, maybe even a few more dinner invitations.

---

60   Kardas, M., Kumar, A., & Epley, N. (2022). "Overly Shallow?: Miscalibrated Expectations Create a Barrier to Deeper Conversation." *Journal of Personality and Social Psychology*, 122(3), 367–398. https://doi.org/10.1037/pspa0000281

In my experiences at conferences or social events where I am the newcomer, I strive to apply the Intention to listen and learn. Rather than simply networking, we can build genuine connections and Reverberate by aligning our Presence with the Intention to engage with others. Further, we can align our Story with our Presence and Intention by seeking to discover and appreciate other's stories and facilitate introductions. This approach enhances the experience and encourages a richer exchange for everyone involved.

 **TIPS AND TRICKS**

How to ace a first conversation with a stranger by Reverberating:

1. Review your Personal SOI. Let it be a reminder of how you want to show up. If there is someone you would like to meet, create a specific Intention for that conversation, too.
2. Arrive prepared with a story or two you are comfortable sharing with a stranger. You may feel more prepared if you practice it aloud.
3. Leave the weather to the weather reporters. Small talk is fine in the first minutes but dig deeper as the conversation moves along.
4. Do more of the talking with strangers you want to get to know. Be encouraging and inquisitive but remember they are feeling unsure, too.
5. Be willing to be transparent about sharing what has heart and meaning.

CONFLICTS IN CONVERSATION

Disagreements are a normal part of communication. As

a child, I remember many times when my sister and I argued, screaming at each other until my mother sent us to our rooms and then later made us apologize once our tempers — and voices — had simmered. Invariably our disagreements were about simple things — what television program to watch or who got to play with which toy — but they all boiled down to a difference in opinion. As children, we would revert to yelling because we had yet to learn more constructive mechanisms for resolving conflict.

One can hope that maturity means that we scream less often and are not sent to our rooms, but there are still plenty of times when adults have conflicting ideas and devolve into the same childish behavior. A quick scroll through any social media platform will provide a multitude of examples of how not to reconcile differences of opinion. When that happens, people tend to become emotional, and when strong emotions enter the picture, communication becomes difficult, if not impossible.

Conversations sometimes fail because communication is hard. We have created a culture in which people who disagree with each other either avoid conversations all together or dive straight into blame and judgment. But despite the difficulties, it is exactly at this time when we need to embrace constructive conversations to gauge and understand our differences and to figure out how we can bridge the divide. And if bridging isn't possible, then to simply accept and respect our differing points of view.

When we have strong disagreements, communication can feel especially impossible. It requires a special kind of Presence to navigate through an impasse. When faced with deeply opposing views, it's essential to commit to bringing empathy and compassion to the conversation. However, this can be particularly challenging when we are dealing with grief, shame, or horror.

That's why I am inspired by the work of Azim Khamisa and Ples Felix. In 1995, Azim's son was murdered by Ples' grandson during a botched robbery attempt while Azim's son was delivering pizzas in San Diego. Although Azim was devastated by the loss of his son, he turned to his faith and recognized that there were victims on both sides of the tragedy. He reached out to Ples and expressed that he held no animosity toward him or his grandson. Azim had already established the Tariq Khamisa Foundation in memory of his son to promote forgiveness, and he invited Ples to join him in this mission. Today, they speak together publicly to help prevent youth from joining gangs.

I firmly believe that if Ples and Azim could bridge such a significant divide, then anyone can. First and foremost, it requires the Intention to heal by suspending judgment and by remaining open to others. The Story we share must reflect this openness and compassion. When we embody a Presence that aligns with our values, when we "walk our talk," we can create ripples of positive change, Reverberating even in extreme situations. Better yet, others can Reverberate as well.

TIPS AND TRICKS

Even in conflict we can seek to align our Intention, Story, and Presence by keeping these five basic concepts in mind:

1. **Start by agreeing.** Find something on which you can agree such as shared experiences and common concerns. For example, we can all agree that we want to be happy, that we want the best for our children, that we are tired of arguing, or that things are not right.

2. **Be genuinely curious.** Ask clarifying, open-ended questions without blame or judgment. Stay away from closed-ended questions, ones that can be answered with a simple "yes" or "no." Sincere curiosity is reflected in a quizzical Presence and an open cadence. When that is mirrored in questions that demonstrate listening and interest, Story and Presence reflect the Intention to learn and understand.

3. **Practice empathy.** Let go of your Story enough to step into the other person's Story. Sometimes it's challenging to stay receptive. It's helpful to know what our reactive mode looks like and to realize we all do that differently. Mine is defensiveness, and though I sometimes fail to be as open as I intend, I believe it's important to continually work to be responsive rather than defensive.

4. **Show respect and civility.** Practice intellectual humility. Certainty is a psychological trap. Avoid attacking the person or their beliefs and instead focus on the issues at hand. This kind of Story can help foster a more productive and constructive dialogue.

5. **Be open-minded.** It is important to approach difficult conversations with the Intention to keep an open mind and a willingness to consider different perspectives. To align our Presence with our Intention and Story, we can show genuine interest in others by leaning into the conversation, by meeting their eyes, and using affirmative body language, no matter how different their thinking is from our own.

The kind of conversation described above is not one with a conversational Intention to persuade or cajole. Instead, the overall conversational Intention is to begin to converse with someone with whom we disagree or have had an argument, to stop the divisiveness and get back to a place where we are able to hear each other even if we agree to disagree. It may not be a quick fix, but by actively listening, showing respect, finding common ground, asking questions, and being open-minded, we can foster more productive and constructive dialogue.

HUMOR, IMPLICITNESS, AND INQUIRY

It can be difficult to know what will make a conversation meaningful, but even in the most difficult situations there are three ingredients that can contribute to effective communication whether at home, the office, or any place in between, even a video conference. The three ingredients are humor, inquiry, and implicitness. They involve emotions and empathy, which as we have seen are critical to impact and provide options for how to show up and what to say. They can also be illustrative of a frame of mind.

Let's take a look at each and how to find the appropriate balance to Reverberate in even the most difficult conversations.

HUMOR

Humor is a powerful spice. Like any spice, too much can have bad effects, but when used in the right proportion and at the right time, it can add the perfect flavor to any meal.

When I was growing up, our family would engage in conversation over dinner. It was one of my favorite times. We would hear stories, share experiences, express feelings, and even have heated debates. That's right, we would disagree and then discuss our differences! Imagine such a world. My dad was often the instigator as well as the facilitator.

Dad loved to play devil's advocate. He would take on contrary positions and have us defend our views with reason and evidence, though we often would slip in heavy doses of emotion and passion, which was accepted and encouraged. These dinner conversations certainly helped me to shape my own views about life, but it wasn't always fun. Sometimes we got our feelings hurt. When this happened, my dad would lighten the mood with well-placed witticism or a silly dad joke.

Today, I recognize his use of humor as a way he Reverberated in those situations. His Intention was never to harm but to teach, and though he insisted that we all show up to the conversations by holding them at the dinner table, he stayed present enough to know when it was time to stop teaching and recognized that relationships transcended winning.

Today, when I have a difficult discussion, I look for the opportunity to inject humor to rise above the conflict and ease into a better place, even if only temporarily. Comedy writer Nikki Frias, author of *Does This Divorce Make Me Look Fat?* says that comedy is universal and sheds light on the similarities we face every day.[61] To learn more about the power of humor, I took a webinar with her in 2022. The class was short, but I liked her style and I asked her if I could interview her for this book.

When I questioned her about humor alleviating tension, she said: "There is a natural tension that people have conjured up within themselves based off daily stress and anxiety and things like that, and humor allows people to just breathe or catch their breath. Going to work, going to the gym — all these things that we have in our lives build up to create tension. I think sometimes just cutting that tension by providing humor in your natural state is so beneficial."

Nikki feels humor can make us more receptive to each other. She said, "I always tell people that humor is my superpower because of the amount of response and openness you get from people when you are just so comfortable...I can laugh at myself, I can make fun of myself. Not everything has to be so serious."

Humor can take the edge off of a tense situation because it has a soothing effect on the brain. In her book, *Humor's Hidden Power: Weapon Shield and Psychological Salve*, Nichole Force writes: "Among other things, laughter has been shown to reduce stress, boost the immune system and enhance brain chemistry through the release of serotonin and endorphins."[62]

---

61   Frias, Nikki. *Does This Divorce Make Me Look Fat?: A Self-Help Guide To Getting Over It Already. Seriously B*tch.* Nikki Frias, 2022.
62   Force, Nichole. *Humor's Hidden Power: Weapon Shield and Psychological Salve.* Braeden Press, 2011.

Force also describes how humor has helped people through such horrible times as the Holocaust.

And just in case we need more reasons to justify using humor, Milan Kundera, author of *The Unbearable Lightness of Being*, has been credited as saying, "It's because a person has a sense of humor that we feel we can trust them." Additionally, I submit that the Story element of humor must align with a clear Intention to do no harm and an authentic Presence for us to trust the humorist, and I agree that laughter is good at easing tensions.

IMPLICITNESS

We all know the feeling of the elephant in the room: when there is a looming question that everyone is aware of but perhaps too polite to ask out loud. We also know that if left unattended, that elephant can quickly become highly distracting and even destructive. The truth is, if we deny what is unsaid but known, we miss an opportunity to foster deeper connections. When we evade the truth and fail to share from the heart, we perpetuate falsehoods and plant seeds of mistrust. We also waste a lot of energy and time talking around what is important rather than dealing with it.

Assuming the former, and our conversation is fraught with avoidance of what everyone knows needs to be addressed, one solution is to be direct. Just how direct depends on the culture. In Western societies, being painfully direct can be curative; in Eastern societies, it's best to be diplomatic and respectful of prevalent social conventions.

I have a colleague who is a communications professional in the Middle East. One of the biggest lessons he learned is that what is left unsaid is often heard more clearly than what is actually said. When he crafts communications, he puts as much time into thinking about what is being left out as he does on what is being *included*.

The elephant in the room can have a significant impact, but just as humor that targets another person can lead to negative consequences, implicitness can result in discomfort, confusion, and even resentment. As adults, our individual Theory of Mind — an essential tool that allows us to infer others' Intentions and understand discrepancies between words and visuals — plays a crucial role in navigating implicitness. When a lack of alignment leads to miscommunication, our Theory of Mind can help us recognize what remains unspoken.

What about those times when managers must withhold information from employees? This lack of openness often leads employees to speculate about what is implicit, and rumors can begin to circulate. A client of mine named Joe, an executive at a large tech firm, was on a flight to Poland for a site visit where he anticipated being asked about the extensive layoffs that had just been announced. Discussions about the layoffs had been ongoing for a month, and while the final decisions were starting to crystallize, they were still subject to change. Joe was frustrated with how the company handled the situation — by informing the media about the layoffs before notifying their own employees and without a clear plan in place. However, as part of the executive team, he felt compelled to remain silent until the plans were finalized.

Joe found himself concerned about how to address these issues. He had set the expectation that he would be honest and open, but he knew he wouldn't be able to share much information about the situation. Thinking about his high-performing team, he realized they deserved more than a refusal to address the topic or, worse, dishonesty, which some of his colleagues had resorted to. He opened his laptop, started a document, and began crafting an Intention for how to respond to the anticipated questions and how to address the discussion proactively. After half an hour, the final version was as follows:

> *"My Intention is to be open and honest about what I can and can't share with my employees, so they leave our discussion feeling they can trust me to care about them while also doing what's necessary for the company's survival."*

After settling on that statement, he scheduled Zoom "office hours" for the coming weeks, during which he would be available to answer questions as they arose.

The next day, Joe gave a presentation about the company's

current state and how his organization was faring overall. After finishing his slides, he set them aside, grabbed a chair, and sat in front of the group, inviting questions. As expected, the first question was about the layoffs. People wanted to know what would happen and whether they were safe. He responded truthfully, explaining what he could — though it wasn't much — and shared the dates and times for the upcoming "office hours." He encouraged them to participate in those Zoom calls and assured them that he would always provide information to the best of his ability regarding the situation.

Unfortunately, some employees were on the list to be let go. In the following weeks, a few felt disappointed, fearful, and angry. However, many more were impressed by Joe's integrity and by how his actions aligned with his words. Several employees who were laid off even sent him emails expressing gratitude for his honesty. Joe later shared with me that crafting his Intention made all the difference in that challenging situation. It helped him stay focused and enabled him to engage with his team as he intended, even when he faced the difficulty of not being able to share everything that was going on.

Ultimately, the question of implicitness depends on the situation, but for impact it should be addressed. As we've seen, there are circumstances in which leaving things unsaid is the best option, and some where Reverberation happens because we speak up. In either case, it is important not to ignore the unspoken.

INQUIRY

I tend to see the glass half full. When in conversation, I assume the other person is well-intentioned, even if the conversation is difficult. Sometimes I'm disappointed, but I prefer to agree to disagree rather than believe people are jerks simply because they have a different point of view. This perspective also allows me to be curious and ask questions. I've learned a lot about life, people, and the world around me by being curious. I've also found that people appreciate being asked about their ideas and experiences.

In June of 2024, I was an actor in a play created in just eight days to provide the experience and the example of how curiosity creates connections even when people vehemently disagree. A collaboration between Braver Angels and the New York Theatre Workshop (NYTW) aimed to use storytelling and theater to bridge political divides at the 2024 Braver Angels convention. Braver Angels is a cross-partisan, volunteer-led organization seeking to bridge the partisan divide in the U.S. The New York Theater Workshop is an Off-Broadway theater whose members believe theatre can "deepen empathy and spark wonder."

The initiative adapted NYTW's "Mind the Gap" program. Participants, ranging in age from 14 to 92 and from diverse professional and political backgrounds, auditioned without knowing the exact process or outcome. The final cast included therapists, musicians, engineers, and educators, many with little to no theatrical experience, united by curiosity and a shared commitment to dialogue through the arts.

Throughout our time together, we used theater games to break down political barriers, creating a safe space to connect beyond labels. Through interviews, we used inquiry to discover deeply personal experiences – feeling like outsiders, making life-and-death decisions – then transformed them into short theatrical pieces tackling immigration, free speech, economics, and abortion. These exchanges challenged us to embrace differences, find common ground, and stay open to genuine curiosity.

Long after the convention, the experience stayed with us. Some deepened their commitment to Braver Angels, others became more involved in workshops, but all of us were changed. By the end, we weren't just a cast – we were a family, proving that even in a polarized world, art can build bridges where politics divide, and curiosity can open the door to connection.

There is a lot of blame thrown around when life gets difficult, particularly in politics. Grass-roots groups all over the world arise when this happens, many with the idea of bringing opposing parties together. In the U.S., groups like Braver Angels, It Starts with Us, and No Boundaries became more visible after the contentious 2016 elections. In November 2020, Columbia University's Morton Deutsch International Center for Cooperation and Conflict Resolution published a list of hundreds of these organizations.[63] What many have in common is inquiry as a tool to better understand people with opposing points of view.

Another form of inquiry, "appreciative inquiry," is used to describe a specific process of communication that has had tremendous success, particularly in areas of strife between different cultures. It was created in the 1980s by American organizational development expert David Cooperrider and others. According to the United States Environmental Protection Agency, an organization that uses appreciative inquiry, it is "a systematic process that uses the art and practice of asking questions and building upon stories to foster innovation and imagination."[64] It is a strengths-based approach that uses "the best of what is" to imagine and plan a shared, positive future for all stakeholders. The roadmap used is called the "4-D cycle" and consists of four stages: discovery, dream, design, and destiny. The process has been used to create change in corporations, improve school cultures, and assist members of warring factions in finding ways to work together for peace.

The idea of appreciative inquiry is powerful and can result in more meaningful conversations. To apply the concept, we

63   Columbia University. (2025 November 08) "Organizations Transforming Polarization & Division." *The Morton Deutsch International Center for Cooperation and Conflict Resolution*. https://icccr.tc.columbia.edu/resources/organizations-bridging-divides

64   EPA. (2025 November 08). "Public Participation Guide: Appreciative Inquiry Process." United States Environmental Protection Agency. https://www.epa.gov/international-cooperation/public-participation-guide-appreciative-inquiry-process#:~:text=Appreciative%20Inquiry%20is%20a%20systematic,to%20foster%20innovation%20and%20imagination

must agree to remain respectful and hopeful, with courage or conviction to keep the conversation going. We must remain open to each other with a desire to learn and grow and create something better together. And we must then ask meaningful questions that reflect a desire to understand and imagine together rather than superficial ones that are desperate attempts to fill silent spaces or questions driving to a particular point of view.

The lack of an agreement to learn and grow together is often where inquiry stops. It has been pointed out by cultural and social critics for some time now that the internet, once the haven of inquiry, has become a den of accusation and 'piling on.' It seems when people have the freedom to comment at will without censure and have unlimited access to a broadcast platform, which operates outside the boundaries of accepted social conventions, bad behaviors tend to surface.[65]

It is fascinating to learn that although more than 60% of the world's population are on social media, less than half of all users post content.[66] But many repost what they've seen and that is where the problems of misinformation begin. Thirty-eight percent of views of text misinformation and 65% of views of photographic misinformation come from content

---

65   Anderson, Ian Axel, Gizem Ceylan, & Wendy Wood. (2025 November 08). "Social Media Can in Fact Be Made Better: Research Shows It Is Possible to Reward Users for Sharing Accurate Information Instead of Misinformation." *The Conversation*. https://the-conversation.com/social-media-can-in-fact-be-made-better-research-shows-it-is-possible-to-reward-users-for-sharing-accurate-information-instead-of-misinformation-209676

66   Jones, Jeffrey M. (2025 November 08). "Social Media Users More Inclined to Browse than Post Content." Gallup. https://news.gallup.com/poll/467792/social-media-users-inclined-browse-post-content.aspx

that has been reshared twice, meaning a share of a share of a share of an original post. It is alarming to consider that so much content on social media comes from so few people and perhaps more alarming that the people who share then share and proliferate that content rarely check its validity.

BARRIERS AND REMEDIES TO REVERBERATION

Sometimes we are our own worst enemies when it comes to not Reverberating – failing to establish an Intention, failing to practice, failing to consider our audience or our call to action. Other times, however, the universe seems to conspire against us. How do we identify and overcome barriers to achieving Reverberation?

TACKLING STAGE FRIGHT

I was on stage, the bright lights shining down. As I often do, I felt a wave of happiness for having such a fantastic job. I was singing a song I had rehearsed countless times and loved to perform. What an enviable position! Caught up in the emotion of the piece, I placed my hand on my heart and was shocked to feel it pounding wildly in my chest. I was nervous! I couldn't get my mind off the hammering heartbeats and my fear became more and more apparent.

I scanned the audience. Doubt began to creep in like a thick fog that clouded out the words of the well-rehearsed song and all the confidence I usually felt on stage. Instead, I felt exposed, as if everyone could see right through my facade. I felt like a fraud, trying to convince the world — including myself — that I had something to offer as an artist. It was a moment of sheer terror.

Fortunately for me and the unknowing audience, singing requires deep breaths, and as I took a deep breath, the fog began to clear. I pulled my hand away from my heart and regained my composure. Although it took a few minutes, I was able to overcome the unexpected panic, and the rest of my performance flowed smoothly. Later that night, after the stage door had been locked and we had all gone home, I thought about that terrifying moment and discovered two invaluable truths about stage fright: first, deep breathing can calm your heart rate and help you regain control; second, it's best to avoid touching your hand to your chest while singing or speaking before an audience!

It's hard to Reverberate when filled with fear. Stage fright is a very real issue for many speakers and performers. For those people, just when they need clarity and focus, the mind is scattered, and their head is filled with critical self-talk that can be immobilizing or at least distracting at the very least. The internet is full of ideas for dealing with this situation. Some involve tranquilizers and anti-depressants, while some recommend meditation and perseverance. The latter two are my preference, but are there other choices?

Since observation is critical to continuous improvement and awareness is essential to impact, we need to listen to the voices in our heads, hopefully distinguishing between the critics and the helpers. Stage fright is primarily caused by those critical voices, and sometimes they are so loud that we cannot hear the helpers. Let's try to understand what's going on to better understand how to deal with it.

The feelings of panic or lack of clarity are often due to the increase in adrenaline that is released in the body when in front of people. The effect of this chemical is so strong that in 2007 The Royal Society of Chemistry gave a prize for the most harrowing case of stage-fright experienced in the UK that year. They called it the Olivier Stage Fright award because apparently, Sir Laurence Olivier said he only experienced one such attack in his more than 60 years on stage. But that one was terrible.[67]

On that night, Olivier believed that if anyone on stage had eye contact with him, he would freeze on the spot. The criteria for the award included spirit, innovation, and determination shown in overcoming an attack of stage-fright. With the chemists believing everything can be related to chemistry, the idea was to honor the power of adrenaline to get us through tough situations such as terrible stage fright.

Some studies indicate that both the audience and the performer's psychological makeup have a lot to do with stage fright. The size of the audience seems to matter as does their predisposition to hear what the speaker has to say, with stage

67 Blakemore, Michael. (2025 November 08). "The Day Laurence Olivier Got Stage Fright." *The Guardian*. https://www.theguardian.com/books/2013/sep/17/laurence-olivier-national-theatre-blakemore

fright increasing when faced with a large, hostile crowd. I can certainly understand that. In addition, a high need for approval can intensify the demands felt by a speaker. Again, that makes sense to me since personally, I didn't have stage fright until being on stage meant a paycheck.

However, what I found most appropriate was the work at New York University Medical Center that suggests stage fright is a learned behavior which can be unlearned through a clinical process of desensitization. Not everyone has to go through a clinical treatment program, though. Through repeat opportunities (systematic desensitization) to face the fear, we can become desensitized to the fear of doing what makes us fearful. This is why people who frequently present tend to be less nervous than those who don't.

A wonderful gift of desensitization is that we can turn our fear into our teacher. In his book *Clutch: Why Some People Excel Under Pressure and Others Don't*, Paul Sullivan tells stories of some remarkable people who did NOT let fear get the best of them.[68] The author outlines lessons learned about dealing with fear as an asset rather than an enemy. The lesson about stage fright has to do with learning to be present. If we remember what we are supposed to do and stay focused on the work and Intention, we will spend far less time fearful of what will happen or what others will think. For me, I see practice as an ally in Sullivan's lesson. The more comfortable

---

68 Sullivan, Paul. Cluth: *Why Some People Excel Under Pressure and Others Don't.* Portfolio, 2010.

we are with our material, the more present we can be.

I find I am less fearful when I focus on how I can be of service to my audience rather than focus on what they think of me. I remember everyone wants me to succeed because no one wants to see me fail. That's pretty simple. In exchange, I look for ways in which I can share something that will make their day a little better, even if just for a minute. I believe we all have something to say that others need to hear. To do this we do not have to be experts on anything other than what we know.

 **TIPS AND TRICKS**

5 TIPS TO FEEL THE FEAR AND DO IT ANYWAY

1. Make sure you have eaten before you speak so that low blood sugar doesn't make the adrenaline rush turn into nausea, dizziness, or out-of-control trembling.
2. Instead of thinking that you are fearful, try to see the anxiety as anticipation and excitement. It is a charge that you can use in any way you choose.
3. Be prepared. Get to know as much about your audience ahead of time as possible. Then when you arrive, shake hands, and mingle so that you have a more personal feeling about them. In addition, practice your material over and over until you are sure you know it well.
4. Breathe. Deeply. Breathing will help calm you down and focus. It will also help to remind you that you are in your body, which is another way of keeping you present and in the moment.
5. Instead of waiting to be asked, take more opportunities to speak in situations where you have control. Be prepared to

speak at family gatherings. Volunteer to give presentations at non-profits you support. Go to networking meetings and talk to everyone there. Then, take the plunge and give an impromptu speech at a luncheon you are attending.

 **EXERCISE**

DON'T EXPECT TO WING IT: GET PRACTICING!

Don't expect to wing it when you have a chance to set the tone for how others will perceive you.

- Spend time preparing by practicing aloud at least two or three times before you must present, preferably more.
- Take a breath. Find the joy.
- Use a virtual platform like ZOOM or TEAMS to have a meeting with yourself. Record it, watch it, and see what you think.
- Look for what's working as well as what's not.
- Adjust the lighting and the audio to make sure you look and sound the way you want to and then try out your introduction.
- Review what you recorded and work with it until you are satisfied that it's smooth, clear, and a good representation of how you want to be perceived.
- Stay in the game. Don't be afraid to make a mistake.

Possible Outcomes from Practicing:

- Better diction
- Using fewer filler words
- More inflection and vocal variety
- More clarity in content
- Better storytelling
- Greater impact
- Physical improvement

INEFFECTIVE BREATHING

Although breathing is something we do naturally, it is not always something we do as well as we should. There is a great deal to be gained from breathing deeply and consciously rather than as a necessary reflex. The benefits of breathing for Reverberation are numerous, including a clearer mind to focus on Intention and a calmer, more grounded and conscious Presence.

Navy SEALS, yoga practitioners, athletes, pop stars and opera singers find peace and quiet even in stressful, noisy environments by utilizing various practices of breathing to activate the body's natural relaxation response. This response is a physical state of deep rest that changes our physical and emotional responses to stress. There are other breathing practices to be found online, including some for increased energy, for focus, and for increased lung capacity. Here are a few to try:

- **Box Breathing** (For focus): Inhale for 4 seconds, hold for 4 seconds, exhale for 4 seconds, hold for 4 seconds, repeat 5 times.

- **The 4-7-8 Technique (to de-stress, relax and reduce anxiety):** Sit comfortably in a chair or on the floor and close your eyes. Breathe in through your nose to the count of four. Hold your breath to the count of seven. Exhale through your mouth to the count of eight.

Repeat if desired.

- **Belly breathing (For relaxation and increased capacity):** Sit erect in a chair. Rotate your neck and shoulders to release any tension you may feel. Relax your abdominal muscles as you breathe in through your nose. It will feel as though you are filling up a container in your belly and your belly will expand. Keep expanding all the way up into your lungs. At the fullest expansion of your belly and lungs, hold the air for five slow counts. A long-hold cycle will change the carbon dioxide/oxygen ratio and slow your heart rate and calm you down. Then engage the abdominal muscles as if you are doing a crunch and slowly move the air through pursed lips as if you are blowing out a candle. You can repeat this pattern, counting to 10 with each inhalation and again with each exhalation. To increase lung capacity, increase the count by one more number each day until you have reached your maximum.

- **Bellows Breath (For energy and mental clarity):** Keep the mouth closed and inhale and exhale with quick, short breaths through the nose for 10 seconds. Take a 15-30 second break, breathing normally. Repeat 3-5 times.

REFLECTION
A VOICE IN THE WORLD

I am often asked about "Executive Presence." What is it, and how do we get it? This is before we get into the nuts and bolts of Intention, Story, Presence, and Reverberation. So many businesspeople are chasing an elusive trait that they have seen in great leaders of our time, a trait that they feel they must have to succeed, and a trait they fear is only available to people who are either born with it or possess some carefully held secret skill. I assure you that this mysterious quality is not pre-ordained, and it is not a secret. It is a choice arising out of a greater ability to show up how we want.

This choice, however, requires developing skills and practice. What they mistakenly refer to as "leadership presence" or "executive presence " is, as we have seen, just one aspect of a greater whole. It is Reverberation, an alignment of our Intention, Story, and Presence, that audiences recognize as authentic and inspiring.

To achieve this, we must become aware of our surroundings and practice empathy for those in it. We must become aware of how we show up to the physical experiences of breathing and heartbeat, and we must practice being responsive rather than reactive. We must become mindful of our choices regarding how we interact with our environment and its people. Similarly, we must take the time to create an Intention and live into it.

Finally, we have to have something to say. We need Story,

or stories, that align with our Intention and how we show up. None of this happens by accident. It is the result of choice – the choice to practice, harness Story, and grow with it. Reverberation is not easy, but it is achievable, learnable, and available to everyone willing to work for it.

Being willing to share from the heart takes courage and commitment, but the rewards can be great. But most of all, there is no one else on the planet with a voice quite like yours. It's as unique as your fingerprints, and you have something to say. Let your voice be heard. The world is waiting for you to show up.

Reverberation Plan

Bringing Your Voice to Life in the Moments that Matter

1. DEFINE THE MOMENT

Identify the communication situation you want to prepare for.

- What is the occasion?

(e.g., keynote, pitch meeting, team conversation, difficult discussion)

- Who is your audience?
- What is at stake?

2. CLARIFY YOUR INTENTION

Get crystal clear on your purpose for the plan.

- What do I want them to **think**?
- What do I want them to **feel**?
- What do I want them to **do**?
- In one sentence, state your **Intention** for this moment: "My Intention is to…"

3. CRAFT YOUR CORE STORY

Use Story to deliver your message with emotional resonance.

- What story (personal, client, cultural, metaphorical) best supports your Intention?
- What is the takeaway or emotional "hook"?
- What truth does my Story help illuminate?

Optional Tools:

- Try a "memory palace" or "story spine" structure (Once upon a time… Until one day…)
- Map your story to the Hero's Journey if appropriate.

4. EMBODY YOUR PRESENCE

How will you show up physically, vocally, and emotionally?

- What tone or energy do I need to bring?
- How will I prepare my body?

(e.g., grounding, breathwork, warm-ups)

- How will I center my voice?

(median pitch, pacing, clarity)

- What physical setting or visual support will help reinforce my message?

5. ALIGN FOR IMPACT

Bring Intention + Story + Presence together in practice.

- Rehearse your delivery while checking alignment:
  - Does my voice match my Intention?
  - Does my body support my Story?
  - Do I feel my Presence is aligned with the message I'm delivering?
- Identify what needs adjusting.

6. REVERBERATION CHECK

Ensure your message will echo beyond the moment.

- What emotion or idea do I want to linger with my audience?
- How will I invite continued engagement, action, or reflection?
- How will I measure the impact afterward?

OPTIONAL POST-REFLECTION

After your moment passes:

- What worked?
- Where did I feel most aligned?
- What would I do differently next time?
- What Reverberated?

Afterword

If you'd like to explore more insights and resources, visit my website (https://vocalimpact.com). There, you'll discover a wealth of materials to support both your physical and metaphorical voices, including hundreds of blog posts – many featuring links to other publications. You'll also find practical exercises, actionable suggestions, and a collection of concise e-books tailored to specific communication challenges. For ongoing updates and to connect, follow me on LinkedIn: https://www.linkedin.com/in/k8peters/.

I offer dynamic communication impact workshops and provide personalized one-on-one coaching for clients seeking to elevate their communication skills. As a keynote speaker, I'm passionate about sharing strategies for impactful communication and would be delighted to contribute to your next event. To schedule a workshop or speaking engagement, simply reach out through social media or my website.

If you enjoyed the book, found it helpful, and can recommend it to others, please leave a review on Amazon, Barnes and Noble, Goodreads, or anywhere else you find your community of readers. Your comments are always appreciated and will help me get my message out into the noisy world.

Resources

BIBLIOGRAPHY

Alda, Alan. *If I Understood You, Would I Have This Look on My Face?* Random House, 2017.

Bergren, Mark, Molly Cox, and Jim Detmar. *Improvise This!* Hyperion, 2002.

Berger, Warren. *A More Beautiful Question.* Bloomsbury, 2014.

Leonard, Kelly and Tom Yorton. *Yes, And...* Bloomsbury, 2017.

Caesari, E. Herbert. *The Voice of the Mind.* Robert Hale, 1951.

Cooper, Morton. *Change Your Voice, Change Your Life.* Harper & Row, 1980.

Cuddy, Amy. *Presence.* Little, Brown and Company, 2015.

Denning, Stephen. *The Leadership Guide to Storytelling.* Jossey-Bass, 2005.

Dhawan, Erica. *Digital Body Language.* St. Martin's Press, 2021.

Eliot, Marc. *Paul Simon: A Life.* John Wiley & Sons, 2010.

Ertel, Chris, and Lisa Kay Solomon. *Moments of Impact.* Simon & Schuster, 2014.

Estes, Clarissa. *Women Who run With the Wolves.* Ballantine Books, 1996.

Force, Nichole. *Humor's Hidden Power.* Motivational Press, 2018.

Frias, Nikki. *Does This Divorce Make Me Look Fat?* Nikki Frias, 2022.

Guber, Peter. *Tell to Win.* Crown Business, 2011.

Guzmán, Mónica. *I Never Thought of It That Way.* BenBella Books, 2022.

Karpf, Anne. *The Human Voice.* Bloomsbury, 2006.

Peters, Kate. *Can You Hear Me Now?* Narrative Development, 2006.

Ross, Doug, PhD, and Friends. *A Tao of Dialog.* Medicine Bear Pub., 1998.

Rosenberg, Marshall B. *Nonviolent Communication.* PuddleDancer Press, 2003.

Sullivan, Paul. *Clutch.* Portfolio, 2010.

The Moth. *How to Tell a Story.* Crown, 2022.

Tomatis, Alfred A. *The Ear and the Voice.* Scarecrow Press, 1987.

Wood, Patti. *SNAP!* AMACOM, 2012.

NOTE

If you or someone you know is facing a **severe voice disorder** (e.g. vocal cord paralysis, spasmodic dysphonia, scarring, complex laryngeal lesions, neurogenic voice disorders, etc.), you may benefit from a center that has **fellowship-trained laryngologists, multidisciplinary teams** (ENT, speech therapy, neurology, maybe gastroenterology or pulmonology), and **experience with complex and novel interventions.**

Index

A

B

C

D

Acknowledgements

My first approach to writing this book was to take my newsletters, articles, and blog posts and cut and paste them into a manuscript. The result was less than spectacular, which is a big reason why I am eternally grateful to my editor and writing partner, Gary Hernandez. Years ago, I was referred to him by someone who only knew him by reputation. A search online revealed that he was also a marathon runner, a skill he would find helpful in dealing with all my rewrites and changes in direction. We've worked together on multiple projects over the past 20+ years, and I am a better writer for that partnership. It's always been a pleasure!

The look and feel of a book are critical, and I could not have had a finer collaborator in this area than my dear friend, Rick Schank. His artistic vision shaped the cover design and layout, ensuring the book's appearance resonates with readers. He sees what the words say in a profoundly artistic way and cares not only about how the book appears on the shelf but also how it feels to the reader's eye when they look at the page. I am moved by his generosity and his loving spirit.

Everyone with whom I've worked has been a teacher to me. I've learned what I know through my own experience, working with students and clients, and through study and observation. I am grateful for teachers like Dr. Roger Ardrey,

Dr. Maurice Allard, Natalie Limonick, Suzanne Harmon, and Seth Riggs, who taught me about voices and life. My respect and gratitude go to composer/pianist Edward Barnes, pianists Maryanne Brown, Barbara Worsley, Gary Berkson, Shelly Markham, and Sebastian Chang, who have supported me in rehearsal and performance and opened my eyes to new worlds in music. Although I feel it is important not to coach and tell, I am grateful to all those whose stories are included in this book, and for the input from Carlos Pignataro and Tom Tait.

It is not a small request to ask someone to give feedback on your manuscript. Reviewing a book requires reading the whole thing and reflecting on it. For their time and attention to my project, I am incredibly grateful to Jackie Sturm, Mike Sternad, Marjorie McRae, Jane Peters, Debbie Velasquez, Jill Ferguson, Paul Zak, Christina Liem, Wei Li, Kim Kopetz, Laura Browne, and my brother Kamealoha Simao for his help with the Hawaiian quote. I will always be thankful for the faith so many have shown me, but special thanks go to Celeste Romo, Shawna Erdman, Lynn Blough, George O'Meara, and Corinn Crowley.

Big hugs of gratitude go to my talented colleagues, Ursula Kleinecke, a terrific partner who is as passionate as I am about the need for this work, and Melanie Taylor, who trusted me to go on this ride and contributed significant value and lots of fun. Finally, I am grateful to the extraordinary Nubia Velasco, who is always ready to get stuff done, bringing invincible joy and lighting up the world with everything she does.

About the Author

Kate Peters is a highly regarded Executive Communication Consultant and dynamic keynote speaker who has spent decades helping leaders turn their voices into their most powerful strategic tools. The actionable insights in Reverberate! distill her years of guiding senior executives and teams at major global organizations—along with her lifelong background as a performing artist.

Drawing on this unique blend of disciplines, Kate helps emerging and seasoned professionals find their authentic voice, navigate complexity, and spark meaningful change through compelling communication. Holding degrees in both psychology and music performance, she leads immersive communication-impact workshops and provides high-level one-on-one counsel. Kate believes the voice is our most underrated asset, and she's on a mission to help you transform yours into a superpower.